Retire in Mexico - Live Better for Less Money

Dru Pearson

ISBN: 149-6154045
ISBN-13: 978-1496154040

Cover photo of Guanajuato by the author.

This is dedicated to my son Joel who helped me
discover the wonders
of Mexico.

CONTENTS

NOTES

FOREWORD

Six stoplights, a Wal-Mart, a new plaza with a cinema complex and casino, plus a dozen convenience stores now dot the landscape in the little village of Ajijic, but the flavor of old Mexico remains. People still flock to the weekly market; violet, scarlet and tangerine bougainvillea still cascade over the walls like a Christo art installation; the climate still beats any place else in the world; and it is still almost impossible to meet someone who remains a stranger for long. Donkeys still carry firewood on their backs while Mexicans celebrate fiestas with explosions of laughter, music, and fireworks. And, at night, technicolor sunsets are reflected off the expansive lake masquerading as an inland sea. It had been six years since health and family concerns forced my return to the United States, but I discovered, in a month-long visit the summer of 2010, that the heart of the Mexico I remember still beats strong.

My partner David and I had the opportunity to live like expatriates once again when friends asked us to pet sit for them. They offered a two bedroom, two bath house, a terrace and gardens that should be featured in a magazine, a white cat, a computer, and a car. It took us thirty seconds to say yes!

David and I were able to live like expats, enjoy the pleasures again of having a maid and a gardener,shop the markets, and, yes, Wal-Mart, travel the country using public transportation, and talk to old friends and new who still call Mexico home. We had a wonderful vacation, but that vacation also yielded a tremendous amount of information that has been incorporated into the new edition of this book. This updated version of *Retire in Mexico* is the result of that visit in 2010, along with information gained from several more visits to Mexico and lots of input from friends.

I haven't changed the format since I originally wrote this book when I was living in Mexico full-time, but all the information and prices have been updated. There are new links to help you learn more about this fascinating country, personal anecdotes from friends who discuss everything from safety issues to hospitalizations, and, perhaps most importantly, the latest information about the *Visitante* Visa (formerly the FMM tourist visa that visitors receive when they enter the country) and the *Residente Temporal* (formerly the FM-3) the visa that expatriates must have to live here permanently. The tourist and visa changes became law in November, 2012, and were actually implemented in 2013, so this book contains the most timely information available!

Despite the many advantages of retirement in Mexico, some people have been frightened by the reports of violence making daily headlines in the US and Canadian news, but David and I never, not once, felt uncomfortable. Indeed, friends who live here year-round say they feel safer here than they did in their homes back in the States and Canada! We concluded that the reports of violence, although true, are isolated primarily in border cities and do no reflect what is happening in most areas of this vast country where expatriates live. It would be foolish for a European to read the crime statistics for New York or Los Angeles, and conclude that the United States was unsafe to visit; we believe the same thing to be true of Mexico.

When I wrote the first edition of this book in 2003, I promised that Mexico had one of the world's lowest costs of living, a perfect climate in the mountainous central region of the country where furnaces and air conditioners are unnecessary, an exceptionally friendly and welcoming population, and enough social events and cultural sites to keep anyone entertained for a lifetime. Six stoplights, a Wal-Mart, a new plaza with a cinema complex and casino, plus a dozen convenience stores haven't altered those promises. "Progress" has come to "my village" and all other areas of Mexico, but it is still one of the best places on Earth to retire.

1 DECISIONS

On a rainy Friday afternoon, I sat at my desk staring at the figures. Over the past 24 years, I had taught over 3,000 students, read and corrected approximately 28,800 essays, graded close to 30,000 tests, attended 720 teacher-parent conferences, endured 960 faculty meetings, and supervised at least a dozen student teachers.

I turned the paper over and wrote down a few other facts. I would turn fifty in a couple months. My novel, stalemated for over a year, numbered only seven chapters. My wanderlust, always strong, had been sated only once when I spent a summer in Arizona. I probably would have written down a few other discouraging facts if the fire alarm bell hadn't sounded. As I trudged out to the football field with 2,200 high school students and 150 faculty, I knew it was time to change my life. For the first time, I allowed myself to flirt with the idea of early retirement.

It was certainly a radical notion. I'd always thought I'd have to teach until I turned 65 or at least until I'd accumulated thirty years towards a pension. Early retirement meant that I could travel, write, and explore a dozen other interests I kept postponing. The possibilities were intoxicating.

The problem was, of course, that early retirement meant a reduced pension, and a reduced pension meant I would have to find a new place to live. Even though Chapel Hill, North Carolina, was always listed in the top ten of the United States' most desirable retirement locations, it was also one of the most expensive places to live. I would not be able to afford it on a reduced income. If there were an exciting place to relocate, though, the area itself might prove to be part of the adventure.

I decided to look for a place where my dollars could be stretched to the utmost. I also wanted a place with an interesting, preferably foreign, culture, a mild climate, proximity to other Americans and the United States, good health care, and a few luxuries, if possible.

That weekend I went to the library, got every book

available on retirement options, and turned off the phone. I read about southern France--too far away from my family, Costa Rica--the prices had increased considerably in recent years, and Ireland--the gloomy climate would have driven me mad, and by Sunday night, I realized Mexico was probably the most promising place to live.

Before that library visit, I knew very little regarding Mexico. I had heard about its world-class resort areas and Maya ruins with unpronounceable names, but my weekend reading had given me a glimpse of the vast interior region of Mexico. While I certainly wanted to explore the beach resorts, the mountainous middle of Mexico sounded like paradise. It was exotic but within driving distance of the United States. In the places I'd read about there were large pockets of English-speakers living in a few towns. The country's geography varied, yet the people were consistently friendly. The climate in the highlands, where houses required no heating or air conditioning, was among the best in the world. And excellent medical and dental care was available in the larger towns. After I did a few financial calculations, I realized what was perhaps the very best advantage to living in Mexico—according to the prices quoted in the literature, I could afford to have a maid clean my house every week!

I returned the books to the library, got a few others, and made plans to spend my summer vacations for the next couple years in Mexico.

This e-book is the result of that exploration, the actual move to Mexico, and my subsequent experiences in the four years of calling Ajijic (ah-hee-HEEK) home. I will tell you how to choose a location, how to make the transition as cheaply as possible, and how to live in Mexico on a budget while still enjoying some luxuries you could never afford in the States.

But, first, of course, you will probably want to do some thinking about whether Mexico might be the right place for you.

2 WILL YOU BE HAPPY IN MEXICO?

During your working life, a job probably determined where you lived. You may have spent thirty years shoveling snow each winter or railing against the daily commuter traffic but were helpless to do anything about it. But, when you retire, you no longer have to stay in the same place. Perhaps for the first time, you can choose where you want to live.

A lot of people decide that climate will be the determining factor in a retirement location. Florida and the Southwestern states are popular choices, but while the climate may be warmer there than in the northern states or Canada, it is still not perfect. While the winters are pleasant, Florida and the Southwest suffer from extremely high summer temperatures, and Florida's summers are made even more uncomfortable because of high humidity.

Another factor in a lot of peoples' retirement decision

is cost-of-living.   While few people earn as much money post-retirement as they did during their working lives, everyone still wants to enjoy a pleasant standard of living that doesn't involve too many sacrifices.   That is very difficult to do in some of the urban areas of North America.

The Advantages of Living in Mexico

Climate

Living in Mexico can certainly provide you with one of the best climates on earth.   In the highlands, the middle section of the country, furnaces and air conditioners are unnecessary because there are no temperature extremes.   Almost every house in this area has a covered terrace, which becomes the family room.   In fact, outdoor living is so much a part of Mexican living that real estate agents consider any outdoor, roofed area as part of the house's square footage! The only problem with the highlands' perfect climate is that it might get a bit monotonous. The first year I lived here, we had one overcast, blustery, rainy day and everyone was out running errands, thrilled with the terrible weather! L

Luxuries

Mexico is one of the few places I know where you can retire with a 30-50% reduction in your income and not suffer any consequences whatsoever. In fact, you will probably be able to afford new luxuries that might have been impossible during your working life. Since labor is so inexpensive in Mexico, a maid can clean your whole house every week for the same amount you probably spent on a few cups of coffee back home. And with haircuts costing $10-15, one-hour massages by licensed technicians averaging $20, and hour and a half long facials for $21, there's no excuse not to indulge in a little pampering.

Not only can you revel in personal care for perhaps the first time, you can also take advantage of the resorts at reduced prices. The Guadalajara newspaper regularly lists reduced beach hotel rates for expatriates living in Mexico. There are also organized trips sponsored by travel agencies at almost unbelievable prices. During the United States' Thanksgiving week, four nights and five days at an all-inclusive resort in Puerto Vallarta (All your food, drinks—both alcoholic and regular—and entertainment are included.), with first-class bus transportation there and back, cost just $234. They even treat you to a typical Thanksgiving dinner complete with turkey and cranberry sauce!

Healthier Environment

Mexico is also a healthier place to live. No heaters or air conditioners recycle stale air. The tile floors do not retain dust and other contaminants. The windows are always open. The food is the freshest you will find anywhere in the world. And, best of all, you will exercise and not even know you're doing it! Since you have to walk to the post office, browse at the street markets, and stroll down to the plaza to meet your friends, you will be aerobically exercising without even being aware of it. Of course, if you want to join a gym or practice your tango steps, you can do that, too.

Never Boring

I spent 52 years living in the United States, and, while that country certainly has its advantages, it was never as exciting as Mexico. It is almost impossible to be bored here! If nothing else, just driving from point A to point B gives you a lot to look at. Drive down any village street and you will see the "peanut man" or the "watermelon woman" at their roadside tables. Half a block away is a display of wrought iron furniture. Next in line is the family from Oaxaca selling rugs that they've hung from a line strung between the trees. And at the bend in the road, the carpenter has taken advantage of some extra space to display his chairs and tables. Nothing much is hidden in Mexico. It's all out there waiting for you to buy, and the vendor will be almost as happy if you just stop by for a chat instead of a purchase.

At almost any time of day, and on many days of the year, there will be a parade that all the villagers turn out to watch. There are usually one or two or three social activities sponsored by expatriate organizations, too. And at night, especially on weekends, local musicians might be set up on the plaza bandstand while the perimeter of the plaza is ringed with vendors selling tacos and freshly-fried-right-in-front-of-you potato chips.

Even if you stay in your house all day, someone will come to you. The water deliverymen knock on my door every day. I hear the pan pipe melody of the knife sharpener man who will stop and sharpen my dullest kitchen cutlery for a few pesos. And the bell of the garbage truck reminds me to get my trash outside for pick up. Truly, it is difficult to feel lonely or bored in Mexico.

Holidays

There are a lot of holidays in Mexico, usually one or two each month. While all of them are fun to celebrate, I'd like to tell you about two that are particularly meaningful to me.

Christmas

Christmas is a very special time of year. In contrast to the commercialism in most of North America, Mexicans focus, not on gifts, but on companionship. Family and friends take center stage. Friends are invited to dinner instead of being given a gift. While almost every street in the village is decorated with streamers or bells, it is a matter of community pride rather than a show of wealth. All the neighbors on each street decide on a theme for that year, and then spend the day together mounting the glitter to the telephone poles. These decorations would never win any prizes, and indeed the by-laws of most North American neighborhoods would likely forbid them, but here they are a show of cooperation, companionship, and joy.

My first Christmas Eve in Ajijic, my neighbors, Judy, Stan, Doris, John, Ken, Peggy, and I, walked to the plaza around 7:30. We strolled around the brightly lit plaza admiring the handicrafts of the Oaxacan indigenous people, lingered over the food stalls, and stood in awe in front of the nativity scene in the bandstand. Then we wandered over to the village church, the mainstay of Mexican life, a half-block away.

In the church courtyard were children from the village depicting the nativity (nacimiento) scenes in various parts of Mexico and the rest of the world. In one corner the Veracruz Mary and Joseph wore brightly colored robes depicting their more heavily influenced Spanish heritage. Live sheep and goats sat at their sides. In another spot, across the way, were Oaxacans with the baby Jesus in a hammock. And the Arabian manger scene featured children with headbands and long flowing white robes.

The loudspeakers started playing carols, in English, as my neighbors and I made the rounds of the courtyard, wishing our friends-- almost everyone I knew in the village was there--*Feliz Navidad* and best wishes for a Happy New Year.

My neighbors and I sang along with "the carolers" as we walked the two blocks to our houses by the lake, and I felt the spirit of Christmas in a way I hadn't since I was a child.

The Day of the Dead

While the Day of the Dead occurs around the time of Halloween, that's its only similarity with that holiday. It is celebrated in a uniquely Mexican fashion. Because Mexicans believe there are three deaths—the first when the last breath leaves your body, the second when you are buried, and the third and final one when no one remembers you—they make sure to remember their departed ones at this time of year.

On this special day, when the souls of the dead are closer to the earth than at any other time, some friends and I went to the Chapala cemetery. We knew that a lot of families remembered their lost ones in special ways with altars at their homes, but we also heard that every single Mexican considered it a point of honor and responsibility to visit the departed one's grave site. We wanted to see this for ourselves.

As we approached the town, traffic was bumper to bumper. Sheryl found a spot on a side street and we climbed the hill to the cemetery gate. On the cobblestone road outside the entrance, vendors had set up tables roofed with blue plastic tarps strung from the trees. Sweet confections made from honey, sugar cane stalks, and flowers - especially marigolds, the flower of the dead - were available. My favorite table held "dead bread," a rounded loaf of sweet bread dusted with sugar. When the souls came to earth later tonight, their favorite delicacies would be waiting for them.

We walked the uneven paths of the cemetery, stepping aside every couple minutes to let someone pass with a floral arrangement or a bucket of water. We were the only Americans there. While we were reverent, most of the Mexicans smiled and said *buenas tardes*. One old lady even joked and flattered us by calling us senoritas. Everywhere we turned and as far as the eye could see were flowers and young boys, men, old women, and babies in mothers' arms.

We were frequently sidetracked and took crooked paths to exclaim over the sixteen arrangements of roses, marigolds, and gladiolus on one particularly showy grave, or to wonder why a family had mixed both plastic flower arrangements with live roses on another. I kept finding myself counting at each grave. There were sometimes twenty arrangements but never less than five. Some of the more elaborate sarcophagi had floral arrangements such as we buy in the States for funerals. One grave had blue and orange crepe paper banners waving in the air. The two women and girl responsible for the banners were sitting on the ground nearby having a picnic of tacos and Coke. A man a few feet away gave us a shy smile as he paused in his job of whitewashing the base of his family's tomb.

But my favorite part of the cemetery was the area devoted to the poor. Instead of six-foot high marble headstones, these graves had simple wooden crosses with what looked like hand-lettered signs listing names and dates. Most were ringed by a three-foot iron fence, some were covered with freshly mown grass, and all had at least one flower arrangement. Sometimes these flowers were in an old tin can with the label still attached, but as far as we could see, all the graves were decorated.

It seemed appropriate, so Sheryl and I talked about what we wanted for our special "day." For Sheryl it was a bunch of puppies and kittens to visit her grave, while I wanted peanut butter and chocolate. We weren't being the least bit morbid; it was the correct topic of conversation for such a beautiful day. Susan, though, had a different mission.

She had searched hard and long to see if there were any graves left unadorned—a place where no family members were left to decorate and remember. There was only one in the entire cemetery.

Susan placed her blue paper carnation on the iron fence surrounding it. She fumbled a little tying the string and finally wedged it into place. Without saying a word, she looked at us for approval. We nodded yes. It was exactly right.

Elderly Are Respected

Another marked difference between the rest of North America and Mexico is the way the elderly are treated. Here, old people are revered. When a Mexican becomes too old to fend for himself, the family is honored to have him move into the house.

While you would not have a family here to live with if you became disabled or needed assisted living, you would find the same loving concern and care offered in retirement homes. Mexicans consider it an honor to help the elderly and infirm, and the care given is probably better than most places in the rest of North America.

One of my friends moved his father here from a retirement center in Virginia. Bill's career had taken him all over the world, but he was bored living in a small center where the other residents were hometown folks. He said he had no one to talk to. The price here in Mexico, $1200-1500 a month, was half what he was paying in Virginia.

When Bill arrived in Ajijic, he said he immediately felt at home. He loved the weather, and the other residents from many spots around the globe, provided stimulating conversation. When he joined a writing group and began revising his memoirs, he made many friends who were happy to include him in their activities. Shortly before he died at a ripe old age, he said his only regret was not moving to Mexico sooner.

If you would like more information about the many assisted living facilities and nursing homes serving the Ajijic area, this website about Alicia's Center will give you some idea of the quality of living experienced in Mexico. Http://www.aliciaconvalescent.com/ Other areas of Mexico, of course, have similar facilities.

Many Interesting Places to Visit

While almost everyone has heard of the beach resorts in Mexico, few people realize that the country boasts many other fascinating places to visit. David and I met an anthropologist while we sitting in San Miguel de

Allende's *jardin* one afternoon. This woman and her husband had spent a few months in both Buenos Aires and Ecuador, searching for the perfect retirement location where her husband could dabble in his consulting business via telecommuting and she could explore archaeological sites. While they had enjoyed their visits to Argentina and Ecuador, they intended to make Mexico their home, she said, because this country was so rich in culture.

In fact, Mexico has 32 sites, which have been designated by UNESCO as places that must be protected by law because of their cultural and natural importance and significance. Mexico has more of these World Heritage Sites than either Canada (18 sites) or the United States (22 sites). Here's a list of some of these intriguing places and the dates when they were added to the UNESCO list.

1987 Pre-Hispanic City and National Park of Palenque
1987 Historic Centre of Mexico City and Xochimilco
1987 Pre-Hispanic City of Teotihuacan
1987 Historic Centre of Oaxaca and Archaeological Site of Monte Alban
1987 Historic Centre of Puebla
1988 Historic Town of Guanajuato and Adjacent Mines

1988	Pre-Hispanic City of Chichen-Itza
1991	Historic Centre of Morelia
1992	El Tajin, Pre-Hispanic City
1993	Historic Centre of Zacatecas
1993	
1993	Rock Paintings of the Sierra de San Francisco
1994	Earliest 16th-Century Monasteries on the Slopes of Popocatepetl
1996	Prehispanic Town of Uxmal
1996	Historic Monuments Zone of Querétaro
1997	Hospicio Cabañas, Guadalajara
1998	Historic Monuments Zone of Tlacotalpan
1998	Archeological Zone of Paquimé, Casas Grandes
1999	Historic Fortified Town of Campeche
1999	Archaeological Monuments Zone of Xochicalco
2002	Ancient Maya City of Calakmul, Campeche

To learn more about these sites, go to this web page http://whc.unesco.org/en/list and click on whatever interests you. Of course there are many other places in Mexico that are interesting to visit; so many that it would be impossible to list them all. The country has 210,000 registered archaeological sites alone! There are two, though, that deserve special mention because they're particularly unusual.

The state of Michoacan, home to the unique cities of Patzcuaro, Morelia, and Uruapan all of which are worth a visit, is also the wintering spot of the Monarch butterfly. You've undoubtedly seen pictures of this yearly phenomenon when millions of butterflies congregate here to rest on everything they can find, turning the trees and carpeting the ground orange. While the butterflies are protected by law and access to their wintering habitat is limited, it is possible to take a tour of the area to see this amazing sight for yourself. Tony Burton, a local tour guide, has written an article about this experience at http://www.mexconnect.com/mex_/travel/tonysarticl es/monarchbutter.html For further information on the Monarchs, see http://www.monarchwatch.org/

For a place that features giant concrete butterflies that you can walk on, consider visiting the former home of Edward James, Las Pozas, located near the small Mexican village of Xilitla. Influenced by Salvador Dali, Bertolt Brecht, and Aldous Huxley, this rich and rather eccentric brother of writer Henry James spent twenty years of his life and five million dollars creating a surrealistic landscape that rambles across acres of jungle. There are stairs that lead nowhere, flowers with 20-foot leaves, and concrete waterfalls. In all, there are 36 structures, some over 100 feet high, in this extraordinary place. When you visit, you can stay in one of the houses James built on the property or at one of the hotels in the village. For more information about this truly amazing fantasyland, consult this website.http://www.mexconnect.com/mex_/travel/mkernan/onemansfantasy.html

Misconceptions About Mexico

For some reason I have yet to understand, the North American press usually describes Mexicans in the most unflattering way. Stereotypes abound and illegal activity, present in any country, is exaggerated.

If you believe the media, you probably think that all Mexicans are lazy. Nothing could be further from the truth. They are the hardest-working people I've ever met and perform many tasks without the modern tools we're accustomed to. The man who owns the convenience store near the San Francisco Plaza Hotel in Guadalajara proudly tends to his business from 6:00 in the morning until 10:00 at night. When I asked if he minded the long hours, he said no because it gave him a chance to meet a lot of interesting people.

The man who installed a skylight for me chiseled

through the 18-inch concrete roof by hand! Jorge showed me his blisters at the end of the day, but nothing could suppress his smile of satisfaction at having gotten the job done.

Mexicans are thought to be dirty but this, too, is another stereotype that has no basis in fact. They are a people that take pride in their personal appearance. Almost every home has what we expatriates call a "Mexican Maytag," a double sink arrangement featuring a rough surface to scrub the clothes and another space for rinsing. On sunny days, you will see clothes hanging from lines mounted on the rooftops. If the home doesn't have an area for clothes washing, then people use the public laundries. For example, in San Miguel de Allende, there is an outdoor area where a dozen "Maytags" line the perimeter of a small, lovely plaza. Women congregate here almost every day of the week to wash the clothes and visit with their friends.

Misconceptions About Violent Crime

When I planned to move to Mexico, I was warned over and over again that I would be robbed, kidnapped, or murdered. The truth is that, unless you drive a Rolls Royce in Mexico City, you are probably safer here in this country than anywhere else in North America. Yes, there are kidnappings, but only of the extraordinarily wealthy who flaunt their money. And, of course, there are robberies and burglaries, but there is a major difference in the crime in Mexico and that of the rest of North America. Here, poor people simply want your property—they do not want to hurt you. Burglars do not carry guns.

One of my elderly friends awoke one night to find a strange man standing over her bedside warning her to be quiet. She was afraid, of course, and began to cough nervously. The burglar got her a glass of water to ease her raspy throat and told her not to worry as he and his friends were just taking a few things!

You will not hear of drive-by shootings or road rage in Mexico because they simply don't exist.

Truly, I never hesitate to walk down a village street at night or to return alone to my home after dark, two activities that used to make me nervous back in my hometown in North Carolina.

Since 2009, the press has reported an increase in drug violence, and judging by the Mexican news reports, this is a significant problem. Still, during David's and my month in the country, we never felt in danger at any time. The only violence we saw occurred at the hummingbird feeders in our garden where the birds ruthlessly chased and dive bombed each other to reach the sugar water!

We saw a reassuring police presence at the airports, banks, bus stations and cities. Perhaps more significantly, of the twenty or so people we questioned about safety, none said they worried about crime. They also confided that they felt as safe or safer here than they would in most US cities.

Everyone takes normal precautions, of course, just as they would if they lived in any American, Canadian, or European city. Visitors often assume that barred windows and doors mean people are plagued by crime, but those bars are the simplified, much cheaper Mexican version of burglar alarms. Burglars in the States are warned away by a sign notifying them of the alarm system, but in Mexico no sign is necessary. The metal bars dissuade anyone from trying to enter a house illegally.

A 2010 article from ABC news explains why Americans are still flocking to Mexico despite reports of violence in the border cities. Martha Lindley, a former chaplain

and lawyer, who's lived in Merida for three years says
she feels, "...as safe here as I did in Seattle."

3 ASPECTS THAT MIGHT TAKE ADJUSTMENT TIME

It's important to remember that there are some aspects of Mexican life that might take a brief adjustment time. While most North Americans feel fairly comfortable in Western Europe, Mexico is probably the most "foreign" of countries in which to make a home. Many customs and practices will strike you as strange at first, but they will soon become part of the fabric of life south of the border that you'll come to appreciate, or at least tolerate.

Mexico is seldom quiet. A band will practice on the street at 5:00 in the morning, there will be a parade at 10:00, and rockets (*cohetes*) go off at any hour of the day or night. The noise used to annoy me, but I became much more tolerant when I learned the reasons for the clamor. The bands have to meet early because they have to get their practice done before going to their jobs. I'm amazed by the dedication of these people who rise before dawn to practice an avocation that gives them no money, only enjoyment. The parades, while sometimes disrupting traffic, are not really nuisances when I remember that I can sit back and enjoy them because I no longer have to race to work. And the *cohetes* serve a religious function. They are set off to open up the heavens so the bad spirits will escape from earth. Although the noise still bothers me at times, this is an idea with which I'm totally in favor!

Of course there are other noises that occur as part of the daily life in a Mexican village. Since most Mexicans do not have cars to drive to stores or telephones to order products, vendors must go to them. The cry of, "*El gaaaaasssss*," can be heard several times a day when the gas cylinder men are making their rounds. "*Agua*" is the cry of the water truck men who will cheerfully deliver the five-gallon plastic containers to your house. And, if you want the freshest vegetables, run out to the street when the vegetable truck rumbles by. My friend Carol says all this noise makes her feel completely alive, far more so than when she lived in her quiet, air-conditioned home in Scottsdale, Arizona.

First-time visitors are sometimes shocked to see so many dogs on the streets, but, then, Mexicans have a more cavalier attitude regarding animals. They are appalled that North Americans allow dogs into their homes! You will certainly see dogs basking in the doorways as you stroll down village streets, but these animals are very well-socialized and wouldn't dream of disturbing their slumber to bother you.

If Mexicans are somewhat puzzled about expatriates' love affair with dogs, at least they tolerate it. Almost everyone I know has adopted a "street dog," some poor abandoned waif that usually turns into the best dog you ever had the pleasure to know. My dog is no exception. Lena was hit by a car and carried home by my neighbors. When I took her in three weeks later, she was emaciated and quickly lost most of her fur. With love and care, however, she has turned into the best dog I've ever known. She taught herself to "stay," sits on command, licks my hand when I cry at sad movies, and is the best companion who's ever shared my home.

Driving down the cobblestone streets might strike you as another challenge you'd rather not have to overcome. They're bumpy, full of potholes, and sometimes mini-boulders appear at inconvenient places. I'd like to say you'd soon adjust to the quaintness of these 400-year-old streets that add such character to the villages, but I can't do that in good conscience. The roads are simply something you'll have to contend with, but at least I can give you some tips on making navigation and parking a little easier.

When driving down cobblestone streets, it's imperative to drive slowly. Very slowly. More slowly than you've ever driven before. If you don't do this, you'll soon find yourself replacing tires at an alarming rate. When you park on these extremely narrow streets, designed for donkeys, not automobiles, park as close to the sidewalk as you possibly can. Even a couple inches can make a difference. If your side mirrors fold in, put them flush with the car every time you park in a village. These precautions will insure that the car you parked will look the same when you return to drive it away.

When I first moved to Mexico I was terrified of scorpions. In fact, I wasn't even sure I wanted to live in a country where such creatures existed. I heard horror stories about children being rushed to the hospital on the verge of death because of one sting. In truth, scorpions here are no more dangerous than the ones in the Southwestern United States, and not nearly as serious as black widow and brown recluse spider bites back in my native North Carolina. If you take a few precautions, you will undoubtedly never have to worry about them at all. See the section on "Scorpions" for some helpful tips.

Something that scared me almost as much as a scorpion was the armed guard. In Mexico, you'll see what look like teenagers toting machine guns and glancing around with a look that says good-heavens-I'm-terrified-of-this-thing-don't-make-me-use-it.
They're everywhere--outside banks and *casas de cambio*, in front of the drugstore, outside the jewelry store, and beside the ATM machine. Supposedly they are there to protect my money or my future jewelry purchase, I suppose, from falling into the wrong hands, but while I've learned to tolerate these young gun-wielding men, I've never learned to be completely at ease around them. My suggestion is not to let them scare you, but don't stop and chat with them either.

Not for Everyone

While it is true that Mexico is not for everyone, it just might be the perfect place for you. It is definitely a foreign country full of exciting sights and sounds with enough familiarity to make you feel comfortable. If nothing else, it deserves your consideration as a retirement possibility, and I doubt that you'd ever regret an exploratory visit.

4 LOCATION POSSIBILITIES

While there may be a few expatriates scattered in a dozen villages throughout Mexico, most Americans and Canadians settle in one of five locations: the Pacific beach towns, Guadalajara, San Miguel de Allende, Oaxaca, or Lake Chapala. Each area has its own charms and only a visit will tell you which is the best choice for you.

Mazatlan

Most people choose places to live below the imaginary line marking the Tropic of Cancer. To the north of this line, Mexico is mostly dry and desert-like. But south of the line, the true tropics begin with lush vegetation and a more favorable climate. Mazatlan is the first large city south of that line. Because of its coastal location, though, it has high temperatures and humidity. If you think you can handle the hot, sticky summer weather, this area has a lot to offer.

This town was my sister and brother-in-law's first introduction to Mexico, and they fell in love with the country based on what they saw here. They were awed by the pristine beaches, entranced by the little convertible taxis, and amused by the friendly beach vendors who urged one and all to, "Buy my junk."

Of course, they saw only the tourist area, but if they had looked a little farther, they would have discovered comfortable residential districts where expatriates can live relatively cheaply. The full-time resident can enjoy phenomenal sport fishing, first-rate seafood, superb golfing and miles of inviting sandy beaches. In comparison to some other places in Mexico, it's also the least "foreign-feeling" town, and many North Americans find that appealing.

For more information on Mazatlan, see this site which is maintained by a couple who are permanent residents. Http://www.maztravel.com

Or try this one with information for visitors and permanent residents. http://www.mazinfo.com/

Puerto Vallarta

Puerto Vallarta was once a sleepy fishing village but is now a world-class resort studded with great restaurants and entertainment of all descriptions. It's also a city with widely varying sections. The newest area, Nuevo Vallarta, consists mostly of time-share condominiums, marinas, and restaurants. PV itself, where the mountains seem to come down almost to the sea, has two different sections--the new town and the old. The new section is much like Nuevo Vallarta with condo complexes lining the beach, but the old section is where the character of the original sleepy fishing village is best preserved.

In this area, where streets snake up and down the mountains and graceful bridges span the Rio Cuale, you will find art galleries, boutiques, and the houses where Richard Burton and Elizabeth Taylor once lived while filming *The Night of the Iguana*. Here, in a section of the old town called Gringo Gulch, is where most expatriates live.

Gringo Gulch is located near all the shops and restaurants. It would be quite easy to live in this neighborhood without a car because everything is within easy walking or busing distance. While it may be slightly more difficult to find reasonable accommodations here, the higher rent may be offset by savings from not having to maintain a car.

Puerto Vallarta, like Mazatlan, is truly beautiful with roads that switchback their way to the mountaintops to provide views of the azure ocean below. Jungle restaurants, reached only by dirt roads, are nestled in the hills. At night, the sound of church bells will lull you to sleep.

PV also has activities to please the most varied tastes. You can spend your days snorkeling, fishing, scuba diving, golfing, shopping, horseback riding, or bungee jumping, to name only a few.

But, don't forget that the summers can be sweltering. If you've got your heart set on a beach home, make sure to visit in June, July, or August to make sure you can tolerate the weather.

See this site for more information. Http://vallartablog.com

Baja

Baja, the peninsula that juts down into the sea from California, is similar to other beach areas along Mexico's Pacific coast. Because much of it is north of the Tropic of Cancer, however, it has a more desert-like flavor. There is no particular expatriate community there, but, rather, several towns that seem to attract gringos.

If the Baja area is more to your liking because of its proximity to California, USA, Bill Seavey runs some interesting budget tours to the San Felipe area. Approximately four times a year, he will guide you across the border or drive you across in his vehicle for a small additional fee. He either provides free accommodations in his house or helps you find inexpensive lodging.

While in San Felipe, Bill gives you information about solar construction and alternative building ideas. Since he built his own solar-powered straw bale house, he is a man who knows what he's talking about. He can also help you with almost anything else, from finding inexpensive and excellent dental care to giving you information on property for sale in the area. At the same time, he promises you time to have some fun exploring the area.

Consult his website for information about solar energy.

http://www.powerfromsun.com/index.htm

http://amzingforums.com/forum1/SUNDOG/forum.html Visit Don Humphrey's message board site to have your questions answered about Baja.

http://www.todossantos-baja.com/ This site tells you about Todos Santos, close to Cabo San Lucas but worlds apart in living style.

Guadalajara

"The City of Roses" is home to the two things most expatriates think of as being most typically Mexican— *mariachi* music and tequila. Stroll down any city street or head for one of the many plazas and you will hear music played by a roving band of musicians. Stop in a restaurant, and if the owner is in a good mood, you may be treated to a shot glass of tequila!

Expatriates who live in Guadalajara seem to thrive on big city life. The 30,000 or so Americans and Canadians who live there enjoy almost a hundred religious, civic, philanthropic, and social organizations catering to their needs. They have access to modern malls, multiplex cinemas, theater, ballet, opera, museums, a planetarium, and parks. If an illness disrupts the daily routine, there are excellent hospitals, 24-hour emergency pharmacies, and superb doctors to handle any crisis.

And, unlike the coastal towns, the weather in Guadalajara, as in most of the highlands of Mexico, is as close to perfect as it's possible to get. *National Geographic* supposedly once praised this area as having the best weather in the world. While I haven't been able to substantiate that, those who live in the region believe it to be true.

No house, be it a cottage or a mansion, has an air conditioner or furnace because they are unnecessary in this climate. Temperatures rarely exceed 85 degrees or fall below 40, flowers bloom all year 'round, and trees never lose their leaves. The lack of humidity makes even the rare ninety-degree day much more tolerable. And, just like Camelot, during the rainy season from June through October, it usually rains only at night!

Enjoy the perfect weather and see the beautiful historic district of Guadalajara by taking a romantic horse-drawn carriage ride. The *calandrias* leave from three locations: outside the Regional Museum on the corner of Liceo and Hidalgo, the San Francisco Temple located at Corona and Prisciliano Sanchez streets, and the San Juan de Dios market. You can take a half-hour or one-hour ride for a modest fee.

If you haven't tried the delicious tequila manufactured in this area, hop the Tequila Express train on Saturday for a visit to the Herradura tequila factory. For more information about all the tours, both private and public, see this site http://tequilasource.com/distillerytours.htm

If you decide to explore Guadalajara as a possible future home, be sure to stop by the American Society of Jalisco (Amsoc) located in the beautiful tree-lined area of Chapalita. This group will help you get acclimated to Guadalajara, supply you with all the information you need about the nuts and bolts of daily living, and invite you to join them in one of their many social gatherings. http://www.amsocguadalajara.org/

San Miguel de Allende

San Miguel, a UNESCO World Heritage Site, is arguably the most beautiful of all Mexican cities. Because the government considers it a national monument and no new buildings can be added that would destroy the character of the town, the cobblestone streets meander up and down the hills past ancient houses with twelve-foot solid wood doors. It reminds me of an Italian hill town with a distinctly Mexican flavor.

The *jardin*, called in other towns the plaza or *zocalo*, is the true gathering spot for everyone who lives in *centro*—the central residential and business district. Here, people watch the hundreds of noisy black birds called grackles leave the trees in the morning or return at precisely the same time every evening, or they catch up on the news with their friends.

More than any other city, perhaps, San Miguel de Allende is home to the arts. The Instituto Allende was founded in the late 1930's, and its world-famous reputation draws artists from all over the world. *Bellas Artes*, housed in an old hacienda just a couple blocks from the *jardin*, welcomes students interested in art or dance and regularly sponsors exhibits open to the public.

The *Biblioteca*, a library sponsored by North Americans, has more English-language books than any other library in Mexico. In addition to having the most books, the *Biblioteca* also boasts a charming café and an auditorium for lectures and movies. Every Sunday, the library offers tours to people anxious to see some of the beautiful homes in San Miguel. Here, for 250 pesos, you can ride a bus with a volunteer guide and ooh and ah at the splendor hidden behind stone walls.

There's a lot to do in San Miguel. During the day, you can take almost any class you can imagine, from beginning Spanish to advanced tango. At night there are many restaurants and nightclubs catering to North American tastes, or you can sit in the *jardin* and listen to the *mariachi*. If you want to explore the surrounding area, you can tour the historic town of Dolores Hidalgo, home of the Mexican Revolution, thirty minutes' drive away; visit the World Heritage designated area in Queretero; or see the fascinating "tunnel" city of Guanajuato, another World Heritage site, both just an hour's drive from San Miguel.

While San Miguel has a lot to offer, it does have a few disadvantages. It is a little more difficult to reach than other expatriate towns. The major airport is in Mexico City, a four-hour bus ride away, while the much smaller Leon Airport is one and a half hours distant. It is also colder here in the winter because of the 6,500' altitude. There is no organized group of expatriates to help you make the transition to Mexico, although there are many informal ways to get help. And, if you like the beach, it is a long nine-hour drive away. Still, this city is definitely worthy of your consideration.

Oaxaca

Oaxaca is as different from Guadalajara as it's possible to get and still be in the same country. It is more reminiscent of Central American countries than Mexico. Because it was isolated for so long by a wall of mountains, very little has changed since the city fathers laid down the streets in the early 1500's. The two plazas making up the *zocalo* contain dozens of wrought iron benches and one of the most impressive bandstands in Mexico. Here people gather to eat in one of the many restaurants ringing the *zocalo* or to look at the wares being offered by the traveling merchants.

Indigenous people make up a large part of the population, and it's not unusual to hear the Zapotec and Mixtec dialects spoken. But even though you may not be able to speak Spanish with the locals, you will undoubtedly be amazed by the works of art they create. Oaxaca is known as the art capital of the country. One of the Rockefellers had a huge collection of Mexican art which was purchased mostly in the Oaxaca region.

Here you will find whole villages devoted to the creation of custom-woven rugs made from hand-carded wool and dyed naturally with fruits and berries. In another place, every family has at least one artist who creates fanciful, brightly painted woodcarvings called *alebrijes*. A guide can direct you to the town famous for black pottery where the color results from the clay that is used, not a slip that is applied.

If you have a hankering to explore history, Monte Alban, a city that thrived before A.D.1000, is a short drive away. The beaches of Puerto Angel, Puerto Escondido, and the newly developed resort area of Huatulco are accessible in a few hours. San Cristobal, another fascinating mountain town in southern Mexico, is also worth a visit.

But what is it like to live here? The weather in Oaxaca is similar to that of Guadalajara, so in that respect it is quite a pleasant place to live. The North Americans, numbering below 600, seem to like their isolation and have not formed an expatriate group. Most seem to prefer immersing themselves in a truly Mexican town, rather than limiting themselves to a mostly expatriate community. The city is also quite a long way from the American border, so it would add several days' drive if you plan to return to the States or Canada frequently. Still, this is a fascinating place to explore, whether you end up relocating here or just visiting.

http://www.oaxaca-travel.com This site provides a lot of information on Oaxaca.

http://www.realoaxaca.com Stan Gotlieb has lived in Oaxaca for seventeen years and shares his insider information and observations here.

Mérida

Mérida, capital city of the state of Yucatan with a population hovering around a million, is an increasingly popular spot for expatriates. Like Oaxaca, geography originally prevented the walled city from being influenced by the rest of Mexico, so it has retained its unique personality.

While the city is justifiably proud of its Maya roots and distinct accents (Spanish is spoken with an accent you won't hear anywhere else in the country while a significant portion of the population still speak a Yucatec Maya), modern amenities abound. Museums, art galleries, fine dining establishments, and boutiques pepper the landscape noted for its pastel mansions and white limestone public buildings.

Today, Mérida's historic center, is the second largest in the country (only Mexico City's is larger), and many expats are buying the rundown mansions to restore. For the story of one couple's restoration, see this blog http://www.imaginemerida.com/?page_id=1474. To read about the cost of living in Mérida, see this site http://www.yucatanliving.com/yucatan-survivor/the-cost-of-living-in-merida-yucatan.htm

Lake Chapala Area

When I made my exploratory visits, I concentrated on San Miguel de Allende, Guadalajara, and Lake Chapala. Oaxaca, in the southernmost region of the country, was simply too far away, and I rejected Mazatlan and Puerto Vallarta because I knew that I would not be able to tolerate the heat and humidity of a coastal town's summers. San Miguel de Allende came close to winning my heart with its colonial charms, but for me, the Lake Chapala region, and, in particular, the village of Ajijic, was the best choice.

Lake Chapala is the largest lake in Mexico, measuring some 25 miles in length. It is ringed by mountains and tiny towns reached by modern roads. At 5,000 feet, the climate is unbeatable with temperatures seldom falling below 60 or rising above 85 during the day, little humidity, a rainy season from June to October when it usually rains only during the night, and ever-blooming flowers and trees.

Not only is the climate almost perfect, but the location

is ideal for other reasons, too. The international airport is just thirty minutes from Ajijic, between Ajijic and Guadalajara. A taxi to the airport costs $30, but friends are usually willing to drive because the airport, on the outskirts of town, is easily reached via a four-lane highway. Guadalajara, the bustling city of close to six million described above, has historical buildings, many outstanding cultural events, excellent medical care, a zoo, parks, regional markets, and all the stores we are accustomed to in our native countries: Wal-Mart, Costco, Sam's Club, Office Depot, and Home Mart (similar to Home Depot). If you head in the other direction from Guadalajara, you can be, in just 2 ½ hours, in Colima, a delightful university town surrounded by coconut palms, or you can reach the beach in only four hours.

But, of course, these advantages would not be enough if there were no other Americans and Canadians in the area. While no one seems to know the exact figure, most people estimate that there are about 10,000 expatriates living in the Lake Chapala/Guadalajara region. Most are full-time residents while some live here only six months of the year, returning to their native countries in the off-season. Having so many expatriates means that there is some planned activity--

or two or three--every day of the week.

But what really convinced me to move to Ajijic was the sheer natural beauty of the place. Four of the rooms in my house overlook my terrace where perimeter planters hold purple and red bougainvilleas, a periwinkle plumbago, yellow-bearded iris, a huge bird of paradise and lots of ferns. When I walk my dog, I frequently marvel at the mountains, unspoiled by urban development, spiking the azure sky. The orange flowered tabachine trees and the bougainvilleas spilling over garden walls add color to every street in the village. Truly, everywhere you turn, the scenes remind me of Impressionist landscape paintings and each season has its own surprises.

While bougainvillea and roses bloom every month of the year, there are certain trees that create a spectacular spring with a riot of color. The lavender jacaranda trees, similar to the wisteria vines of my native North Carolina, lace the sky with their delicate flowers and carpet the sidewalks with their purple petals. In April, the orchid trees put on an amazing show, producing hundreds of orchids on each tree. I was pleased when my plant at home produced six blooms, but now I find myself living in a place where whole streets are lined with thousands of orchids.

http://www.youtube.com/watch?v=eXBkjiiSLbU This you-tube video shows you the Ajijic farmers' market.

http://www.ajijicnews.com/ This site lists all the events and shares the news of Ajijic.

http://www.lakechapalasociety.com/ For all the information pertinent to expatriates.

5 CHOOSING YOUR LOCATION

While there are some people who come to Mexico for a week's vacation and end up living here for the next twenty years, most people adopt a more prudent course and do some homework first. Here's what I recommend. Make a list of likely places to explore. Only you know what is most important to you, but be realistic and focused.   Don't be tempted by imagining your hammock slung between two coconut palms if you know the beach's 98-degree temperatures in the summer would leave you dreaming of air conditioning. Choose places to visit that meet your needs.

How to Get Around

All the major airlines fly to the international airports in Mexico, and the relatively new Volaris Airline provides a low-cost alternative from US border states. David and I were delighted one summer with our pleasant flight and the price. Our Volaris trip from Tijuana's airport to Guadalajara was $400 cheaper than any other airline.

I don't recommend driving for your exploratory visit to Mexico, but if you choose to do this, please see the sections on "Crossing the Border" and "Driving in Mexico." Once you're in the country, I highly recommend taking the first-class buses to get from city to city.

In the United States it is much more common for people to drive their cars, rather than take a bus. The bus system is therefore very limited. But the reverse is true in Mexico. Fewer people have cars so almost everyone uses the bus. The result is that the public transportation network is extensive, and the prices are low. You will not be disappointed with a first-class bus in Mexico.

Riding a first-class ETN or Primera Plus bus is unlike any bus experience you've had before. These luxurious vehicles pamper you with reclining seats, enough legroom to satisfy the tallest basketball player, air conditioning, panoramic windows, movies, refreshments, bathrooms, and, in some cases, a hospitality bar dispensing coffee and tea.

Any travel agent in Mexico can make the reservation for you—you choose your seat assignment in advance—or you can usually get a seat by going to the bus station itself. I highly recommend the first seats on the passenger side of the bus. The windows are larger and the leg room even more accommodating.

The price for a first-class bus is also quite reasonable. I traveled round-trip from Guadalajara to San Miguel de Allende for less than $65; from Guadalajara to Puerto Vallarta and back for around $70; and took a short, one-hour, round-trip from San Miguel de Allende to Guanajuato for less than $15. This website will give you ticket prices and other travel information. http://www.etn.com.mx/english/

In smaller towns, you can use the local bus for three or four pesos or jump in a taxi. Both are inexpensive and efficient ways to get around.

Cabs in Mexico are quite reasonable and ubiquitous. I think there are as many taxis in San Miguel de Allende as there are in Manhattan! An added bonus is that a tip is not expected. Of course, if the driver lugs your 50-pound suitcase into the trunk, you might want to give him a few pesos. Generally, 25 pesos will take you from one side of the city to another, with rates being much lower if you're only going a short distance. At night, there's often a slight increase in rates, and the price is also higher if you call a cab to pick you up at the hotel rather than hail one on the street. Since most taxis are not metered, it is important to agree on the price before you get in the cab. Just tell the driver where you're going and ask, "*Cuanto*?" If the price seems too high, ask another driver for his best price.

Hailing a cab on the street is good practice in small towns, but, please note, however, that in the large cities such as Mexico City or Guadalajara, or at the major airports, it is imperative to arrange for your taxi by going to the official taxi stand. There you will tell the manager your destination, pay the fee, and get a receipt. The manager will arrange for the next taxi in line to take you where you want to go. .

If you want to travel very cheaply for only a few pesos a ride and experience Mexico as a native, ride the local buses. The local bus network is extensive because that's the way most Mexicans travel. If you stand by the side of any Mexican road long enough, a bus will rumble by and pick you up! The destination of the bus is usually printed on the windshield banner, but you can also check with the driver by saying in a questioning tone, "*Autobus a mercado*?" (Does this bus go to the market?) Almost any query preceded by "a" (pronounced ah) will elicit a "*si*" or a "*no.*" It is also important to have the exact, or almost exact, change. Most drivers will not accept bills, but can give you small amounts of change called *cambio*.

This might be a good time to mention that I traveled extensively throughout Mexico for three summers knowing five words of Spanish, and I had a wonderful time! Unlike Europeans, most Mexicans know very little, if any, English, but somehow, with pantomime and a phrase book, I was able to make myself understood. Of course, I realized only later my mispronunciations probably provided them with endless amusement, and perhaps that's why they were so congenial in return. For example, in Mexico a guest must request the bill be brought to the table at the end of the meal. The wait staff would never be so rude as to imply you'd overstayed your welcome by giving you the bill before you asked for it. Even though I consistently mispronounced "*la cuenta*" when asking for the bill and used a French accent I couldn't seem to shake, my waiters always seemed to understand.

Women Traveling Solo

Not only did I know almost no Spanish, but I also had

the supposed disadvantage of being a woman traveling alone. There were endless queries about my marital status the first year because Mexicans couldn't understand why a woman my age wouldn't be married. I tried explaining about my divorce to a few people, but I could tell that gave them the wrong impression. Divorce only happens to "loose women" in Mexico, and if I were divorced, perhaps I'd like to make some deserving Mexican man wealthy by marrying him! In subsequent years, I wore my mother's old wedding ring and had no more problems.

If you are a particularly young or very attractive woman traveling by yourself, you might also be the object of unwanted attention from Mexican men. The women's movement of the 70s doesn't seem to have made much headway in Mexico. Men will often catcall their approval as you pass down the street, and the men who speak a bit of English won't hesitate to try out their words (lines) on you. It is best to try to avoid encouraging their advances, and you can do this simply by ignoring them. If this is a particularly worrisome thought to you, you might want to buy a cheap wedding band to wear while you're in the country.

Finding Accommodations

Before arriving in Mexico, you've undoubtedly mapped out the cities you want to visit and found accommodations. Frommer's *Mexico, The Lonely Planet Guide to Mexico, or* any of the Moon publications provide excellent, reasonably priced hotel recommendations. Armed with your recommendations, walk into the hotel lobby and ask for a room. Most desk clerks speak some English, so it's not difficult to make yourself understood.

The most important point to keep in mind about most hotels in Mexico, though, is that the rooms in any hotel will vary tremendously. Most are housed in former haciendas so it's unusual to find two rooms alike. It is very important and expected that you will ask to see the room. Don't forget that rooms fronting on the plaza or main street may have a great view but will probably be noisy at night. While the interior rooms may be not as charming, you will probably have a better night's sleep.

To arrive at a price, you might ask for the hotel's best rate. While the government requires all hostelries to post their prices, the manager may give you a lower rate if business is slow.

Remember to Take These Items

If it's essential to you, don't forget to take a washcloth so you can wash your face. All hotels will supply you with towels and a bathmat but almost none will have a washcloth available. A flat plastic drain stopper is also a good item to tuck in your suitcase, especially if you wear contact lens, because many sinks lack the means to keep your contacts from disappearing down the drain. I hope you also remember to take earplugs. Even though you may have a quiet room, a fiesta will keep you awake for hours unless you're prepared. One other thing to remember is that most hotels do not have potable water coming through the faucets. There is probably already bottled water in your room, but be sure to ask the clerk how you can get more if you run out.

How to Handle Money

I hope you decided to use your automated teller machine (ATM) card, rather than Travelers' checks. Remember, Mexico is a "cash society," and most places will not accept Visa or Master Card, let alone Travelers' checks. The only place to cash Travelers' checks is at a bank and that often requires a long wait. ATM machines are plentiful and easy to use, with directions in English. If possible, use the ATM during normal banking hours just in case the machine "eats" your card, or, better yet, find a machine that uses the "swipe" method so you retain the card at all times during the transaction. Before leaving home, it might be a good idea to check with your bank to make sure your daily limit, the amount you can withdraw per day, will be sufficient for the trip. Also tell them not to be surprised that you are withdrawing cash in Mexico.

If you prefer to carry cash and perform the currency conversion when you arrive, you can use a bank or a *casa de cambio*. When you enter the bank lobby, look around for the machine dispensing numbers that will tell you when it's your turn to talk to the clerk, and be prepared for a long wait. A better choice might be the *casa de cambio* where you will usually find a better exchange rate. There will be at least one, if not five or six, *casas de cambio* in each city, centrally located, with no lines. You will receive a little slip of paper showing the exchange rate as a form of receipt.

Once you move to Mexico, you will want to think in pesos, but until you acquire your "peso legs," this method for converting pesos into dollars should help. While the peso exchange rate varies slightly from day to day, it's been fairly consistent for the last several years with ten or twelve pesos being equal to a dollar. That means you can simply drop the last digit from the two or more digit peso amount to convert the sum to dollars. A hotel room costing 350 pesos equals about $35 US. An item for 120 pesos is $12 US, and a 90 pesos dinner costs $9 US. When you drop to single digit pesos, add a zero to convert to US cents. For example, a soda for 5 pesos equals 50 cents.

There's one other invaluable tip regarding money that you must know. Because Mexico is a cash economy, you will have no records of your transactions in your checkbook or on your credit card bill. Since some people have very short memories—I was once asked to pay a week's hotel bill twice--it is very important for you to keep your own records. Very few establishments will volunteer to give you a receipt. One of the best investments I ever made was $1.29 for a receipt book. When I ask for a receipt and the clerk looks befuddled, I whip out my book and politely suggest he use it. No one has ever refused.

Where to Get Information

When you are exploring a city as a place to live, there are certain places you should go to get information that no tourist bureau can provide. First, find the *jardin*, *zocalo*, or plaza. It's called different names in different parts of the country, but it's the town's gathering spot. Usually centrally located, this little tree and flower-filled oasis will have a church on one side street and a city government building on the other and lots of restaurants and shops in between. Sit on one of the benches among the trees and talk to people. Expatriates, so called because they choose to live outside their own countries, not because they are unpatriotic, love to be asked why they chose to live in this particular town. Their answers can help you make your own decision.

If the town has an expatriates' association or an American Legion, by all means plan to spend several hours there. In Ajijic, the Lake Chapala Society (LCS) on 16 *de Septiembre* has an office dispensing information six days a week from 10:00-2:00. You can also buy a cup of coffee and a pastry at the snack bar, sit on the Society's patio, and talk to a dozen people about Lakeside.

You will be amazed at the delights to be found at LCS. The buildings and beautiful grounds were donated to the expatriate community by Neill James, an intrepid traveler and prolific writer. Here you will find a video library, an English-language library, a reference room, and a free mail service. Consulate, insurance, and Social Security representatives, doctors, and nurses all make regular visits to the center to help the members with problems or health concerns. Lectures and classes are held in the outdoor gazebo or the Neill James sala. To learn more about LCS, visit their website. http://www.lakechapalasociety.org

Neighboring Chapala holds the American Legion. Stop by their lovely facility on Morelos Street, enjoy a meal in their restaurant, and kibbitz with other expatriates. In Guadalajara, head for the American Society of Jalisco in the Chapalita neighborhood, the American-Canadian Club, or the American Legion or Ladies Auxiliary where the city's expats socialize. While San Miguel de Allende has no formal expatriate center, you will find Americans at the Biblioteca (library run by Americans and Canadians), the Bellas Artes (an organization devoted to the arts), and the Instituto Allende (an excellent source for art lessons and information).

No matter whether you have a religious preference or not, a church is a good place to learn about a community. Attend the service and see how many people welcome you and invite you to brunch afterward. Read the local newspaper. Almost every large town in Mexico has an English-language paper. And, if you're feeling adventuresome and want to get an overview of the whole town, jump on a local bus and check out the local neighborhoods. All of these methods should help you get a feel for the place that's right for you.

6 LEARNING MORE ABOUT MEXICO

When you return home, keep "in touch" with Mexico and learn more about it by accessing Internet magazines, English language newspapers, and by participating in discussion groups. The best on-line magazine, available for free, is http://www.mexconnect.com. There is a wealth of informative articles you won't find anywhere else and a very active web board where you can post your questions and receive excellent advice.

The websites listed below have no subscription fee, unless noted, and offer lots of information.

For general information about Mexico, visit these sites:

http://www.mexconnect.com As mentioned above, Mexconnect is considered to be the best source of information and advice about Mexico on the Internet today.

http://www.peoplesguide.com/ *The Peoples' Guide to Mexico,* by Carl Franz and Lorena Havens, is considered by many to be the classic source for Mexican information. Carl and Lorena now live in Ajijic and maintain a lively website.

http://www.mexonline.com/ This site has lots of general information regarding Mexico.

Http://www.focusonmexico.com This site offers an informative, free newsletter and tours of Mexico. While the emphasis is on the Lake Chapala region, much of their information and advice applies to the entire country. This is a valuable resource.

Http://www.mexicoguru.com Offering the latest information on airlines and public transportation plus many other helpful bits of advice, this site is extremely helpful.

The following are English language newspapers or newsletters about Mexico:

Http://www.bajatimes.com This news magazine serves Baja.

Http://thenews.com.mx/ Published in DF (Mexico

City.)

http://www.oaxacatimes.com For those living in Oaxaca.

Http://www.atencionsanmiguel.org/ Serves the San Miguel de Allende area.

Http://www.lajerga.com Bills itself as, "The only independent bilingual alternative newspaper in Mexico."

http://mexicofile.com This is, according to the website, the insider's guide to living in Mexico.

Http://www.mexperience.com A free newsletter about all things Mexican.

Http://www.gringogazette.com A fee-based newsletter. One year's subscription costs $26.

For information about specific places in Mexico, try one of these sites:

These two links take you to English language magazines that are published in the Chapala area.

http://www.ajijicnews.com/

http://www.lakechapalareview.com/

http://www.chapala.com/chapala/ojo.html

http://www.chapala.com/wwwboard/webboard.html This is where you can ask questions about Mexico and get answers from people who live there.

http://www.theguadalajarareporter.com/ The English language newspaper in Guadalajara.

http://www.lakechapalasociety.org/ The Lake Chapala Society whose mission is to help expats make an easy transition to Mexico.

http://www.chapalaguide.com/ Published by Teresa Kendrick, this guide lists all sorts of useful information for the newcomer to Lakeside. The website contains a list of Ajijic restaurants.

Http://www.virtualmex.com There's a treasure trove of information about many areas of Mexico.

http://www.realoaxaca.com/ Stan Gotlieb tells you what it's like to live in Oaxaca.

http://www.canadianclubmx.com/ This site contains information about the Canadian Club in Ajijic.

For personal narratives about moving to Mexico, see these sites:

http://rollybrook.com/Page%20Directory.htm   Rolly's account of his life in Lerdo, Mexico. Rolly is an active participant on Mexconnect forums, and his website is packed with information.   He has also recently collaborated on a book about living in Mexico.

Http://www.maztravel.com This is one couple's site on living in Mazatlan.   There's a lot of information here.

The next eighteen links take you to blogs that recount the personal experiences of people who made the move to Mexico, settling in Ajijic, San Miguel de Allende or the state of Michoacan (the cities of Morelia and Patzcuaro).   Exploring these pages could keep you entertained for months!

Http://www.vivavida.us

http://mexico-with-heart.com

http://ontheroadwithgary.blogspot.com/

http://mexicowoods.typepad.com/mexicowoods/

http://www.fallinginlovewithsanmiguel.com/gpage1.html

http://www.mexico-with-heart.com/2003/san-miguel-de-allende-where-americans-abound/

http://travelwithsally.blogspot.com/2009/07/morelia-heart-of-mexico.html

http://www.mexicocooks.typepad.com/

http://eddiesayshola.blogspot.com/

http://billiemercer.blogspot.com/

http://jesusdelmonte.blogspot.com/

http://mexicotrucker.com/

http://www.steveinmexico.blogspot.com/

http://tzuru4.blogspot.com/

http://travelswithtravis.blogspot.com/

http://zocalodemexicanfolkart.blogspot.com/

http://mexicodailyliving.blogspot.com/

Here are some links to articles about Mexico:

http://barrygolson.blogspot.com/2010/04/barry-golson.html   Barry Golson, writing for AARP, an association dedicated to issues affecting people over 50 years of age, explored different expatriate areas of

Mexico. He and his wife so loved what they saw that they built their own house on Mexico's Pacific Coast in Nayarit!

http://www.aarp.org/entertainment/books/info-2006/gringos_excerpt.html   The Golson's home building experience and transition to living in Mexico is related in the book, *Gringos in Paradise*. This link leads to an excerpt from that book.

http://www.latimes.com/business/la-fi-zchapala21oct21,1,7445849.story?ctrack=1&cset=true This article from the *Los Angeles Times* newspaper recounts the experiences of gringos who move to the Lake Chapala area.

http://travel.nytimes.com/2009/12/27/travel/27hours.html If you only have 36 hours in San Miguel de Allende, this article from the *New York Times* newspaper will help you make the most of it.

http://www.nytimes.com/slideshow/2009/12/25/travel/20091227-MIGUELALLENDE-SLIDE-SHO_index.html A *New York Times* slideshow.

http://www.nytimes.com/2008/11/21/greathomesanddestinations/21expat.html   Another *New York Times* article about San Miguel de Allende.

http://mexicomyspace.ning.com/profiles/blogs/lake-chapala-vs-hawaii   Kristina Morgan compares the geography and cost of living in Mexico and Hawaii. She concludes that Mexico is as idyllic as Hawaii but has a much lower price tag.

If you'd like to explore Mexico and want to do some camping, there's a superb site you won't want to miss:

http://www.ontheroadin.com/mexicocamping.htm
This is the best place for camping advice in Mexico. This comprehensive site describes the campground, gives direction and price, and usually includes a photo.

If you choose to move to Mexico, these websites will keep you in touch with the government in your home country.

US Government websites

http://www.1040.com/   This site supplies all the information and forms you need to complete your income taxes. The downloadable forms are acceptable to the IRS.

http://www.ssa.gov/   This is the official Social Security website. The "Questions About" search feature will answer any question you have.

http://www.travel.state.gov   Here are scores of documents relating to every travel question imaginable.

http://www.servicecanada.gc.ca/   This site supplies information about Canada's old age security and pension plan.

http://www.ccra-adrc.gc.ca/menu-e.html   Need to know about your tax responsibility when you are an expatriate? Look no further.

http://www.carp.ca/ The Association of Retired Persons will give you lots of advice about moving out of Canada.

7 MEXICAN PAPERWORK

The laws regarding visas changed in November, 2013, and, as is often the case in Mexico where it takes everyone a few months to figure out how to interpret new laws, they were not enforced routinely until about February, 2014.

For me, finding information about the laws and the new visas was an exercise in frustration. Because I now live in Tucson, Arizona, just sixty miles from the Mexican border, I naively assumed my local consulate could help me understand the laws. I explained my mission and submitted my request via e-mail and telephone message.

A response came three weeks later via an early morning phone call. Since this information would be published in a book, the consulate was waiting for the Minister to rule on what information to dispense.

Weeks later, I finally got dozens of links to the regulations. All in Spanish. All unable to be translated via the usual computer-translator methods. Explaining to the consulate representative that I could not read Spanish proficiently enough to interpret these legal documents did no good.

I finally visited the consulate in person, not mentioning my book, and got some answers. That information, coupled with reports from friends dealing with visa issues, and lots of information from various websites and blogs, means the information you're about to read is the most accurate and up-to-date available.

My experience also points to a truism about Mexico. You may be stymied by red tape and baffling roadblocks, but, if you are patient and try to find other ways to get around the problem, you will most likely succeed.

Having spent a great many weeks researching this information and even longer trying to understand all the new rules so I can explain it to you, I have learned that the new rules really do expedite the process.

Here is what you need to know.

When you've chosen your perfect place to live in Mexico, you must next decide what type of permit to get so you can live there. After you've lived in Mexico for a while (at least one year) you may want to consider applying for a *Residente Permanente*, but in the beginning your best choices are two, a *Visitante* Visa (formerly called an FMM or an FM tourist visa) or a *Residente Temporal* (formerly called an FM-3).

Visitante Visa

You receive a *Visitante* automatically when you enter the country. For example, if you were vacationing in Cancun, you would be given this type of visa. It requires no paperwork and involves a 306 peso fee (about $25) if you are driving across the border, or it is included in your airline ticket if you're flying. By the way, do not lose the visa as it's impossible to leave the country without it. However, it allows you to remain in Mexico for only six months, and then you must cross the border to obtain another *Visitante* for another six months'stay.

Many people live year-round in Mexico by returning to their home countries every six months and then renewing their *Visitante* when they return. Snowbirds who choose to live in Mexico only half the year find this the perfect solution. For those who want to live in Mexico year-round, however, this approach has a few drawbacks.

It is impossible to keep a car in Mexico permanently with a *Visitante* or to import your household belongings without paying customs. This car restriction is a recent change; now that the Mexican government has entered the computer age and tracks your car and you, it is impossible to keep your car in Mexico once your visa expires. If you do, you risk it being confiscated by Mexican officials. Also, importing furniture with this type of visa is prohibitively expensive because of customs fees.

If you choose to use the *Visitante* visa by crossing the border every six months with only the household goods that will fit in your vehicle, you can live in Mexico full-time. This is what you must do to also make your car "legal."

To drive your car into Mexico, get your Temporary Import Permit (TIP) when you get your *Visitante* visa when crossing the border. The permit costs $48.84 and is available at the border, from your Mexican consulate, or from the *Banjercita* website at https://www.banjercito.com.mx/registroVehiculos/

Along with the $48.84 fee, you are also required to pay a deposit which ensures that you will remove your car from Mexico when your TIP expires. It ranges from $200 for cars 2000 and earlier to $400 for cars 2007 and later. Owners with cars ranging in age from 2001 to 2006 pay $300.

When you drive your vehicle back across the border to the USA every six months to renew your *Visitante,* you should perform an extra step to ensure you can return to Mexico with your car. Before you cross the Mexican border, stop at *Aduana* (customs) or *Banjercita* and obtain a permit to allow the car to leave and enter Mexico multiple times. If you do not plan to return to Mexico with your car, then you should stop at *Aduana* to have the import sticker removed. Also at this time, the deposit you charged to your credit card, either $200, $300 or $400, will be applied back to your credit card.

If you do not plan to maintain a car in Mexico or bring many of your belongings, you might want to consider this visa; however, it might be problematic and expensive for you to leave and re-enter the country twice a year. To learn what household goods you can legally bring into the country in your car with this visa, see this website.

http://yucalandia.com/answers-to-common-questions/what-can-i-bring-into-mexico-mexican-customs-rules-the-article/

Residente Temporal

The other option for living in Mexico for a long period of time (one to four years) is to obtain a *Residente Temporal.* Most expats opt for this visa, but it also has its limitations. After four years you must either transition to the *Residente Permanente,* which allows you to live full-time in Mexico with no annual paperwork renewals, or you must cross the border to your native country and begin the process all over again at your home state or province Mexican consulate for another four-year *Residente Temporal.*

There are, of course, some advantages to having the *Residente Permanente* quickly (You do have to have a *Residente Temporal* first for one year) since you can work and receive all the rights of a Mexican citizen except voting rights and certain capital gains advantages, but I think you are wiser, in the beginning, to choose either the *Visitante* or the R*esidente Temporal.* Even if you are convinced Mexico is the best place to live, circumstances involving your health or your family may make leaving inevitable. Also, I think four years (The R*esidente Temporal* is available for one, two, three or four years all at once. Or you can renew the visa every year for four years.) gives you enough time to know if you and Mexico are a good fit. The honeymoon will be over and you will have had enough time to experience the highs and lows of living in this wonderful country. You will know if Mexico is the place you want to make your forever home.

*S*o, let's assume you have rejected the six-month Visitante Visa and have decided to apply for the longer *Residente Temporal.* Here's how to go about it:

Step One: You must begin this process in your home country or in any country in which you are a legal resident. For a list of the consulates in the USA and Canada, along with their telephone numbers and addresses, see this link.

http://www.mexonline.com/consulate.htm

It is advisable to go to the consulate office in person; it is extremely difficult to accomplish much over the phone since you will need to fill out paperwork. Still, if you have a general question, you may want to call them. Use the link in the paragraph above for the phone number.

Consulates vary on the items you must present when applying for the visa (My Tucson office requires only three items.), but it's wise to be over-prepared rather than lacking some essential piece of paperwork.

Here are the items you should take to the consulate, and, as is always the case when dealing with Mexican officials, it is wise to have the originals and at least two copies of each. Valid passport; two front and one right profile passport-size pictures, with no jewelry or glasses and with hair pushed back from the face; the payment fee of $36 (May be cash, debit or credit.); your birth certificate; your marriage license, if appropriate; your address in Mexico if you know where you will be staying; and your proof of income.

Nothing about the list above is puzzling except the proof of income requirement, but with a little thought, you can understand why this is necessary. Understandably, the Mexican government does not want a person moving to the country who cannot support himself, so they want you to prove you can afford to live in Mexico and, it is hoped, enrich the economy. The government was quite lax about this requirement in years past, but they enforce it more strictly now.

The income requirement formula is that you must earn 400 times the basic minimum wage in Mexico City. The amount varies a bit each year (The minimum wage increases each January.), but it is roughly $2000 a month for an individual and $2500 for a married couple (A married couple will always pay the base amount plus 50%). To prove that you earn this amount, you must submit bank account statements for the last six or twelve months (The number of months depends on your particular consulate's requirement.)

In lieu of proof of monthly income, the financial requirement can also be met by submitting the original, along with copies, of your proof of investments or bank accounts with average monthly balances equivalent to 20,000 days of general minimum wage in Mexico during the last twelve months. That amount in 2014 is roughly $100,000.

While I would never suggest doing anything illegal, I know people who were so anxious to move to Mexico that they fudged a bit to meet the necessary requirement. Because they missed the minimum amount by only a few hundred dollars, they moved enough money from their savings account to meet the checking account minimum balance, made a copy of their statement, and then moved the money back to their savings account.   They did this for as many months as needed until they had reached the number of months' records their consulate required.

Step Two: Take all this documentation to your local Mexican consulate, pay the $36 fee, fill out the forms and make note of any passwords you are given. When the consulate has approved your application, they will attach a form to your passport that allows you to enter Mexico as a future resident. You will have 180 days to complete your move to Mexico.

Step Three: After you arrive in Mexico, you will have thirty days to finish your application process at the local Immigration (INM) office. According to the Ajijic Legal Immigration office, this process is called *canje*. Before you go to the INM office, make sure you have completed the forms you got at the consulate in your home country when you started this entire procedure (Always have several copies of everything. Do not ever rely on the Mexican government officials to copy anything for you.) and additional passport-style photos. You will also need proof of your address in Mexico along with a utility bill (This does not have to be in your name.); proof of income (Can be the same you used back at the consulate.); birth certificate and marriage license, if appropriate; your passport (original and don't forget copies) plus any other visas issued by Mexico to you; and a letter of application.

You can see a sample of this letter of application at this website. You would probably be wise to seek help from an expat office or from friends when filling this out.

http://www.inm.gob.mx/index.php/page/Solicitud_de_Estancia

Now that you are in Mexico, you can also call the Immigration Hotline which is staffed 24 hours a day, seven days a week, for help. The hotline has some English speakers. Dial 01-800-004-6264.

You can also check with the Ajijic Legal Information office which serves the Ajijic/Guadalajara region at 01-376-766-477.   Their   website   is http://www.ajijiclaw.com.

The only other item you need when going to the INM office is cash. While some offices are allowing first-time residents to apply only for a one-year *Residente Temporal* Visa, you should be allowed to apply for all four years if you want to do so. Getting all four years is cheaper and means a lot less paperwork for you and your car. Once again, though, the choice is yours.

The fee for one year is 3,243 pesos, for two years it is 4,559, for three years you will pay 6,154 and four years is 7,294.

Advantage of the New Law

Once you have the official go-ahead from the consulate in your home state or province, you can prepare to import your household belongings with a *menaje de casa*—a list of your household goods (More on this list later.). This is advantageous to you in one major respect. It allows you to move to Mexico with your furniture at the same time you are entering the country to finish your application for the *Residente Temporal*. You no longer have to make two trips to Mexico as people had to do in the past with an FM-3 (one to receive your FM-3 and then another trip to move your belongings), but can now do everything in just one trip.

Car Insurance and Banking

Next, you will need to make decisions about car insurance and banking. Everyone has advice about these two subjects, but I will tell you the easiest and cheapest way to handle both issues.

It is imperative that you have Mexican car insurance.

You will be a foreigner in Mexico, and it will be difficult for you to know what to do in case of an accident. It is far easier to have insurance that will cover the cost of any accident and legal counsel, should that be necessary. I would strongly suggest that you get insurance that will begin coverage a day or two before you plan to cross the border.

While there are numerous companies at each border crossing and in any town you decide to live, one of the least expensive, and possibly the best, insurance is provided by Lewis and Lewis, 2950 31st Street, Suite 140, Santa Monica, California, 90405-3093 USA. 1-800-966-6830 or 1-310-399-0800. The fax number is 1-310-450-0700. They have an Internet site, http://www.mexicanautoinsurance.com where you can access information, and process your application by mail. I was pleasantly surprised to find my Mexican car insurance cost half what it did in the States.

Another company that's highly respected and reasonably priced is Sanborn's Insurance. You can handle all of your transactions by fax. Visit their website to learn about the company and to get many helpful hints about driving in Mexico. http://www.sanbornsinsurance.com

Confusion

This brings us to a frustrating Catch-22 regarding your car's license plate. Most US states require you to maintain US car insurance in order to retain your license plate, but most people do not want to pay for both Mexican and US insurance when they are only driving in Mexico. If you allow your US insurance to lapse, you are supposed to return the license plate.

The problem is that Mexico demands that your car be plated, either with a US or Mexican plate, but it is difficult and expensive to acquire Mexican plates. So, you must keep your US plate to be able to drive in Mexico, yet the US requires you to pay for their insurance even though you are not driving in the States.

There are only three solutions to this problem. One is to obtain an address, using a mail service, in a border state such as Texas and purchase plates from that state. Texas, with a large population that routinely crosses the border, is much more understanding about insurance matters. They will allow you to keep the Texas plate, maintain only Mexican insurance, and pay your renewal fees only when you cross back into Texas.

The second option is to get a plate from South Dakota. No inspection or insurance is required, but you must have a stateside address when you first order the plate. The office will send renewals to any address. Here are the steps involved. Using the Internet, go to the South Dakota Division of Motor Vehicles website. Download the application form. Then call 1-605-677-7123. The office will tell you how much cash is required. Complete the application form, and send the application, your vehicle title, and a check to: Clay County Treasurer, 211 West Main Street, Suite 201 Vermillion, South Dakota 57069.

The only other option is to get a dispensation from your state's motor vehicle department so that you undergo inspection and pay license plate fees only when you return to that home state.

By the way, Mexico does not care if your license plate has expired. Their only requirement is that you have a plate on your vehicle from some recognized state or province; if it's ten years old, it doesn't matter. Lots of expatriates in Mexico have expired plates because they never plan to drive their cars back across the US border.

In addition to planning for your car's insurance, you

also need to decide what to do about **banking**. Some people live here for years using their automated teller machine (ATM) cards to access money from their home state's bank, but that can be costly if your bank charges hefty ATM fees. The other problem associated with this method is that you can only access a certain amount of money per day.

Other people use Allen W. Lloyd's investment firm because there are branches in several cities and the service is convenient. If you'd like information about this company, contact them via e-mail at lloyd@lloyd.com.mx, or find them on the Internet at http://www.lloyd.com.mx. You may also call for information at the Guadalajara office: 52-33-3880-2000. I used Lloyd's the first year I lived in Mexico but soon grew frustrated with the fees charged for depositing and withdrawing money. That is why I think the best and least expensive option for expatriates in Mexico is to open an account with the US chartered Banamex USA in Los Angeles.

Banamex USA is a subsidiary of one of the major banks in Mexico, also called Banamex, and an account gives you no-fee automatic teller machine, privileges. Since you will find a Banamex in almost every Mexican town, using your ATM card to access money is a painless and no-cost method for obtaining cash. Having an account, however, also allows you to cash checks on your account at any Banamex for either pesos or US dollars, and there are no service charges or monthly fees for any of their services.

Some retirees have their pension or social security checks deposited directly to Banamex USA while others have their home banks send a monthly wire transfer. Since my North Carolina credit union provides one free wire transfer a month, and because I prefer to keep some of my income in savings, I perform my own wire transfer on-line each month to get the reserve I'll need for the coming month.

It is best to establish this account in the United States before moving to Mexico. Call their toll-free number 1-800-222-1234 and ask about their "Friendship Program" for expatriates. Be sure to call several weeks before moving to make sure you have the necessary paperwork completed.

You can also establish an account after you arrive in Mexico by dialing 01-800-111-1234 for information. Their website is http://www.ccbusa.com

Note: As of September, 2013, Banamex USA is

opening new accounts only for people living in Houston, San Antonio and Los Angeles, USA. A spokesperson at Banamex USA said he hopes this "pause" in their "Friendship Program" is temporary, so they will be able once again to open accounts for anyone living anywhere in the United States.

Please contact your local bank to see what programs are in place. Since so many major USA banks have joined forces with Mexican banks, it should not be too difficult to find another type of program similar to Banamex USA.

There's probably one other point I should make about banking in Mexico. While your money will be extremely safe in this country where bank accounts are guaranteed by the government, it is risky to deposit large amounts of money in savings accounts because of the chance of devaluation. The best advice is to retain your savings in your home country and only access what you will need from a Mexican bank on a month-to-month basis.

Other Necessary Papers

Before you begin packing, there are a couple other paperwork matters to attend to. Ask your doctor and dentist to supply you with your medical records. Even if you intend to return to your home practitioner every year, it is wise to have these records with you in case of emergency.

Also, you will need your original car title, a valid state registration, and a driver's license. Make at least two copies of each of these documents. If there is a lien on your car, you must have an affidavit from the lien holder stating that you have the authority to import the car to Mexico. Make two copies of this item, too. In order to pay the fee, approximately $25 US, to take your car into Mexico, you must also have a major credit card (Visa, MasterCard, or American Express) issued in the driver's name. If you do not have a credit card, this would be a good time to apply.

If you're taking a dog or cat with you, you will have to get a statement, a "Certificate of Good Health" from your licensed veterinarian testifying that your pet is healthy. In North Carolina this is called a "Companion Animal Certificate of Veterinary Examination," but your vet will know what form to use if you tell her/him you're moving to Mexico. This should be one of the last things you do. Schedule the appointment a day or two before leaving, because the border officials want a recent statement. Actually, Mexico stipulates this statement must be issued 72 hours before crossing the border if you are flying, but they allow thirty days if you are crossing by car. My dog's certificate was issued on 23 June and I crossed the border on 29 June with no problem.

8 PACKING

Because it is costly to ship items across the border, most houses and apartments in Mexico come fully furnished with everything from a can opener to satellite television. You can literally move in with only your clothing and be unpacked in half an hour, feeling right at home.

Most of us, though, have a few cherished items we'd like to take with us so you will have to decide what those are. There are also a few things that are either hard to come by or are very expensive in Mexico, so you will want to keep that in mind as you prepare to move.

These are items that are difficult to find or expensive in Mexico: electronic items such as radios, tape players, computers, electric frying pans; 100% cotton sheets and towels; books written in English; some car supplies such as alternator and air conditioner belts;

and large-size shoes and plus-size clothing.   It is probably better to err on the side of excess, rather than leave something behind that you love.   While Ajijic and many other Mexican towns have consignment stores that can supply you with anything you've forgotten, they often charge full price (The price you'd pay in a store.) for these used goods.

How to Move Your Goods with a *Visitante* Visa

With this six-month visa, probably the least expensive way to move to Mexico is by packing only your car with the essentials you will need. While the dollar amount of goods you are allowed to import seems to change each week, I got around paying customs on everything except my PC computer (laptops, though, are not subject to duty) by saying I was going to camp for six months. On that first trip to Mexico to look for a house, my van was literally packed to the rooftop with boxes and suitcases, but the camping rationale worked beautifully.   And I didn't feel guilty because I was "camping" in the traditional sense of being a temporary vagabond even though I wasn't sleeping under the stars every night.

If you cannot quite fit everything in your car, there is a relatively inexpensive shipping alternative for a few of your items. Contact Craters and Freighters at 1-800-736-3335.

http://www.cratersandfreighters.com/cf/home.do
With 67 locations nationwide, you can probably find an office close to your home. If you're considering a move to Baja, Mexico, the specialists for this part of Mexico are located in San Diego, California. Call 1-888-380-7447 or consult their website http://www.cratersandfreighterssandiego.com

If you're moving with this visa, there are no special packing requirements. You will have to declare your computer and other electronic goods at customs and pay duty, but this is still the cheapest way to do it. Bear in mind these items must be at least six months old. This way, the government is sure you're importing items only for your own use and not for sale. By the way, because the officials will have to check the serial numbers, it is helpful to have electronic items easily accessible.

How to Move with a *Visitante Temporal*

If you want to bring more items than will fit in your car, you can buy a hitch and trailer that you can later sell in Mexico. Or, if you've decided to take everything—including your furniture—you can rent a commercial truck, drive to the border, and then hire a company called a "forwarder" that will ship your goods to Mexico. Note that it is illegal to drive a US or Canadian rented truck across the Mexican border. The third, and most costly option, is to have a shipping company come to your house, pack your belongings, and take it to Mexico.

If Your Books Won't Fit

If you are moving a lot of books, the cheapest way to get them to Mexico is to use the M-bag postal rate. In the United States, you can ship used books for around a dollar a pound. Go to the post office, get the stickers you will need to affix to each box, find medium-sized boxes at the local liquor store, and start packing. Each M-bag will hold three to four boxes, and the post office requires that each bag weigh not less than 11 pounds and not more than 66.

It is necessary to mail these to a Mexican post office, so you need to use a friend's or realtor's address for that purpose. Also, since you want the books to arrive after you do (It takes about six weeks for the shipment to arrive.) so you can fetch the books from the post office rather than have your friend do so, this should be one of the last things you do before you leave for

Mexico.

Don't Forget the *Menaje de Casa*

If you are entering Mexico with a *Visitante Temporal* and a trailer or a professional moving company, you must follow certain packing guidelines because you will have to supply a *menaje de casa* (household items manifest) listing the boxed items for your consulate and also for customs inspection. Remember to ask for your consulate's *menaje de casa* requirements when you first go there to get your visa paperwork.

The *menaje de casa* allows you to bring an entire household's worth of goods and furniture without paying any customs fees, a tremendous bargain. Of course, in return for waiving the fees for this one-time event, Mexico will expect a lot of paperwork in return. As always when dealing with Mexican red tape, it is almost impossible to have too many copies.

Every box you pack has to be numbered, labeled and inventoried. Loose items should be listed separately, as should electronic items with their serial numbers. Then that list must be translated into Spanish and several copies made of both the English and the Spanish lists. (It is best to type this list, by the way.)

Try this web page to see one man's actual *menaje de casa*. http://rollybrook.com/menaje.htm Take all this to the consulate when you take your other papers and pay a *menaje de casa* fee around $130.

If you have arranged to transport your belongings with

a rental truck you drive yourself to the border and then make a transfer to a professional forwarding company for the actual crossing, you might be able to e-mail your packing list to the moving company for a translation. Many companies offer this service as a convenience to their customers. By the way, this is how I moved my household. I drove a Penske truck from North Carolina to Laredo, Texas, transferred everything to a forwarding company, and picked up my rental car before returning the truck to Penske. The next day I drove to the San Antonio airport where I caught a flight to Guadalajara. The moving truck arrived three days later.

While there are several forwarding agencies in the border towns, one I can highly recommend is the LEGO Group (formerly L&L Agency), 1802 Markley Lane, Laredo, Texas 78041-5608. They moved my things, as well as shipped the goods of four friends, with not a single mishap. In the US, they can be reached by phone at 1-956-726-9941/42 or fax 956-726-8186. You can send a query e-mail to legogroupllc@gmail.com

Another company I can highly recommend is located in Ajijic.   The Stroms operate the oldest moving company in Ajijic, have many years' experience in the moving business, and can move you door-to-door, from your old house to your new one, or from the border to any place in Mexico. Their prices are among the lowest. Their informative website can be accessed at http://www.strommoving.com/

Some Packing Tips

While you can find packing materials at any office supply store, they will be cheaper if you can locate a shipping wholesaler. Since you must use a sturdy tape to secure boxes (a plastic packing tape is recommended by most moving companies), and plenty of bubble wrap or Styrofoam peanuts for your fragile items, it will save you a considerable amount of money to buy from a wholesaler.

This is what you will need: sturdy tape, bubble wrap and plastic peanuts, and an assortment of boxes. Never use newspaper as wrapping or cushioning material. Newspaper ink has a tendency to rub off on items it touches and is very difficult to remove.

Please remember that the roads in Mexico are rough so you must pack carefully to avoid having damaged goods. Pack all items securely and make sure your boxes are full so the items aren't jostled, but do not make the boxes too heavy for stacking.

Items You Cannot Ship to Mexico

If you are going to use a commercial truck, at any point, to transport your goods to your new home in Mexico, there are certain items that cannot be included. You may transport these things in your car, but they cannot be carried in a commercial truck.

They are flammable, corrosive or explosive items; alcoholic beverages; acid, gasoline, poisons, or lighter fluid; barbecue butane or propane bottles; fertilizer; paint; matches; ammunition or weapons; nail polish and nail polish remover; liquid bleach; sterno or kerosene; pool chemicals; chemistry sets; fireworks; pesticides; paint thinner; motor or lamp oil; cleaning fluid of any type; live plants (These may not be transported into Mexico at all. Not even in your car.); pornography of any sort; cloth material in bulk, such as sheeting material; taxidermy items; firearms (This restriction includes bullets or any other type of ammunition, empty cartridges, holsters, cleaning equipment, pellet guns, or even toy guns.); drugs, not even aspirin.

A gun will keep you permanently out of Mexico. Should you manage to somehow cross the border with one, if it is discovered, it will get you kicked out of the country faster than you can say John Wayne was a gunslinger.

Do not forget that any new item will be confiscated. Everything you pack must be at least six months old or look as though it's six months old. If you must buy something new, be sure to take it out of the carton, assemble it, and use it several times before you pack it.

Items Which Should Be Transported in Your Car

For security reasons, these items should travel with you in your car: Valuable jewelry; address books and files; financial statements, check books; bonds, deeds, and tax records; coin or stamp collections; computer software and storage files; medicine. Because the heat in a non-air conditioned truck may ruin video tapes, CD's or photo albums, be sure to pack these in your car also.

Three Weeks Before You Move Checklist

1. If you're driving your car to Mexico, make sure you have proof of your Mexican car insurance coverage. Arrange cancellation with your US-based car insurance company to occur a week after you plan to be in Mexico. Make sure the reimbursement check is sent to a friend or relative for deposit to your home bank account. Put your car title in the same folder with your Mexican car insurance information. In another folder, put your passport. Since you will need copies of all these documents when crossing the border, go ahead and make several.

2. Make the appointment for your pet's veterinarian certificate. Remember, this should be done as close to your departure date as possible.

3. Pick up several copies of the "change of address" form at your local post office. Using a mail service is a good idea in the beginning, but you will probably want to get a local post office box eventually. (Please see the section on "Mail" for more advice.) If you'd like to use Mailboxes, Etc., their website is http://www.mbe.com. In Ajijic, they can be reached by e-mail at mbechapala@laguna.com.mx or phone 52-376-766-0647 or fax 52-376-766-0775.

4. Arrange for on-line banking.

5. If you use credit cards, it's probably best to make on-line payment arrangements. Since it takes a couple weeks for mail to reach you in Mexico and a few weeks for your payment to reach the credit card company, your bills would always be past due and incur unnecessary interest charges. If you make arrangements to check your balance on-line and have payments made from your on-line checking account, you avoid the extra charges and protect your credit rating.

6. Call your utility and telephone companies and arrange to pay your bills before you leave. Again, because of the slow mail service, at best you will incur unnecessary charges if you wait for the bills to be delivered to Mexico and at worst you will ruin your credit rating. If it is impossible to pay your bills in advance, buy yourself a little more time by guesstimating what you think you will owe and pay this amount. Another idea would be to leave money with a friend or relative, change the address on your bills to the friend's address, and have your friend take care of these last bills.

7. If you need prescription medicines, don't forget to

get refills.

8. Enjoy your going-away parties!

9 CROSSING THE BORDER

Even if you arrive at 1:00 in the afternoon at the border town where you plan to cross into Mexico, it's best to wait until the next day before dealing with *aduana* (customs). Spend some time going over your route and change some dollars into pesos (The toll roads in Mexico are very expensive. For example, it costs approximately $100 US to drive from Laredo to Guadalajara. You will also want to have enough cash on hand to pay for gasoline and motel rooms. Depending on your destination, you'll probably need $300-500 total.). Do some last minute shopping to stock up on water and snacks—you will need plenty of both because you'll be driving in the desert and water and restaurants are few and far between—and relax.

You will also want to be sure to get an absolute necessity—toilet paper. While you will find enough bathrooms at Pemex stations or restaurants, you will seldom find paper. It's wise to be prepared by buying some of those pocket-size tissue containers to stick in your pocket or purse. It's also not a bad idea to get some antiseptic cleaning solution for your hands in case you do not find soap and water at some locations.

Here are some websites that provide driving instructions. You can also find excellent maps in the Guia Roji brand of road atlases and state maps. While these are difficult to find in the US and Canada, any bookstore in one of the border states should have them.

http://www.mexconnect.com/mex_/dt/dtdrivinglaredochapala.html This web page supplies directions for the Laredo, Texas, to Lake Chapala drive.

http://www.sanbornsinsurance.com/driving_guidebooks.php Sanborn's Insurance Company publishes excellent driving guides which are free if you join their Sombrero Club for $25.

http://www.maps-of-mexico.com/mapquest.htm You can also try Map Quest's on-line Mexican maps.

http://www.tomzap.com/sp_trans.html#signs This is an invaluable website. It will tell you what all the road signs mean. You may want to print this page to keep in your car as a handy reference.

Try to get up early enough the next morning to reach customs before the office becomes very busy. I have friends who believe that 6:00 in the morning, when the shifts are changing, is the best time, but I've never been able to get there earlier than 8:30. You will also want to make sure you don't cross on a weekend or a holiday as the wait can stretch to six hours. Consult the U.S. Customs and Border Protection website, http://apps.cbp.gov/bwt/index.asp for border crossing points, their hours of operation, and wait times.

You must have these items to temporarily import your car for six months to a year with either a *Visitante* or *Residente Temporal* Visa . You should already have several copies of each of these documents. If you do not, make photocopies before crossing.

The original title.

If you do not own your car, you must have an affidavit from the lien holder stating that you are allowed to import the vehicle.

A valid driver's license. Remember, as long as it hasn't expired, your US or Canadian license is valid in Mexico.

A valid state registration.

A credit card in the driver's name.

Valid proof of citizenship with a passport. Note that a birth certificate is no longer sufficient; you must have a passport.

Even though you may find these steps daunting at first glance, the process is not really difficult. Just follow the detailed steps below and you'll have no problem.

Step One (Note that the following three steps are the approach at most crossing points, but a few have the Customs and *Banjercito* buildings at the 19 or 21 mile checkpoint.)

Pay a small toll and cross to Mexico where you will encounter the "stoplight." This is a short stoplight that shows only a red or a green light. It's used throughout Mexican border crossings and at the airports because the government believes it's a completely unbiased way to monitor tourists. You become the master of your fate because you push the button to see which colored light you'll get. If it flashes green, then you are free to go on. If it flashes red, you will probably need to pull over and let the official take a cursory look at your car's belongings. I say cursory because it's usually only a few minutes' stop, but the official does have the right to search the entire car and everything in it, so be prepared and remain calm. As long as you're not carrying contraband, especially drugs or guns, you have nothing to fear.

If you need to stop in Customs/*Aduana*, you will do so shortly. Just follow the signs. At Immigration you will show your visa and passport. If you have anything to declare at Customs, such as a computer, now is the time. The official will look at your declared item(s), note the serial number, tell you the cost of the duty, and you will be required to pay this before proceeding. Note that because of NAFTA trade agreements, the least amount is charged for items made in the USA, Canada, or Mexico. You will pay the most for items manufactured in Japan or China.

Step Two

Take a deep breath and proceed to the *Banjercito*, the car permit office. Although it is quite close to the Customs area and any official should be able to direct you, it is not necessarily easy to find on your own. Don't hesitate to ask the way. Take your folder of car documents, the visa, some water (most of these offices are not air conditioned and the wait can be long), and get in line. If you get into the building and find a very long line (I waited four hours to get my permit) go back to the car and get your dog. The officials won't mind and Fido will be grateful. A camaraderie develops among the people in line, and someone will be glad to hold your place so you can walk your dog or go back to the car and reassure your cat. If you made copies of your documents before you left, you can relax and swap travel stories with your fellow travelers. If you forgot to make photocopies, do not despair as there's undoubtedly a copy machine somewhere in the building.

Step Three

Affix your permit on the inside of the car window wherever you are told to place it. Double check your directions with the parking attendant and proceed along whatever route you've chosen to the 19 or 21 mile inspection spot located on every road in Mexico.

This is a major inspection site with separate lines for trucks and passenger cars. Do not make my mistake and get in the wrong line! There is no longer a red/green stoplight at this point; you will probably be asked only to show your visa. However, the officer does have the right to see everything in your car, or he may ask just a few questions after a quick look inside the vehicle.   In any case, be cordial and patient. You will soon be on your way. While you may encounter a few other inspection offices after this, you will undoubtedly be waved through.

10 DRIVING IN MEXICO

Driving in Mexico is not for the faint of heart. Because most Mexicans are fatalists and believe that what will be will be, they drive with gusto and little thought for the future. Most drivers see stop signs as mere suggestions and passing on blind curves as an opportunity to prove their machismo. But, as long as you don't adopt these attitudes and you try to drive defensively, the trip should be a pleasant one. You will find a beautiful and varied country whose landscape is not marred by fast food restaurants and billboards. There are just a few points to bear in mind.

As much as possible, you will want to take the *cuotas* (sometimes misspelled as quota or something else approximating *cuota*) or *autopistas* (a synonym for *cuotas*) if you're traveling a long distance. These controlled access, four-lane roads will save you endless time and aggravation. Do not try to economize by taking the two-lane "free" (marked *libre*) roads. Since most Mexicans cannot afford the *cuota* tolls, you'll only see another car every couple miles or so. There are usually refreshment stands, or restaurants, and bathrooms at the toll stations which make the driving even more pleasant.

If you have any sort of car trouble, the government maintained "Green Angel" truck will come to help you. These Florence Nightingales of the roads dispense gas and water, change tires, make minor engine repairs, and just generally do whatever you need to get back on the road again. And the best part of this service is that it's free!

Be sure to retain your receipt when you pay the tolls because that is your ticket to more free services. My friends, Ellie and Rich told me two stories about their experiences on the *cuotas*. When they were driving back to Ajijic from Puerto Vallarta, their SUV's transmission went out. The Mexican couple behind them stopped and used a cell phone to request help. A tow truck arrived shortly and towed Ellie and Rich's car about ten miles to the nearest city, but they paid not a single peso to the driver; there was no charge because the fee was covered by *cuota* insurance. All my friends had to do was show their toll receipt. Of course, they did have to pay the mechanic for a new transmission, but they were delighted to have been able to save at least a little on the tow.

On another trip, just as Ellie and Rich were crossing the border, Ellie realized her old nemesis was returning—kidney stones. She told Rich to carry on into Mexico but the pain became so intense they had to stop at a *cuota* rest stop area. They were told to drive a few miles to the next stop where they would find a doctor. This man gave Ellie the shot that relieved her pain and asked not a peso in return. Again, all they had to do was show their *cuota* receipt.

Although the Mexican government obviously invests a great deal of money maintaining their toll roads, they seem to economize in other ways. They must think road signs are a waste of money as they are few and far between. The ones you do see can be a bit disconcerting because your city will most likely not be listed as one of the destinations. Instead, a city a thousand miles away may be printed as your directional sign. For example, in Guadalajara, I follow the road signs for Nogales (some three days' drive away) when I'm trying to access the bypass in a westerly direction. A good analogy in the United States would be driving from New York to Philadelphia by following the signs for Miami. So, it's wise to be aware of the major city nearest your destination, even if it's hundreds of miles away.

Another point to keep in mind is that most Mexicans have at least a couple uses for the left turn signal. It may mean that the person wants you to pass him; he's telling you the road ahead is clear. It could be that the driver is actually going to turn left. Or it could be he's just waving to a friend and wants to flash his car lights, too. If you're behind a particularly slow-moving truck and he signals a left, pull out cautiously, beep your horn, and quickly pass. When making left turns of your own, use your signal and also stick your arm out so the person behind you will have no doubt about your intentions. In some small towns, it is wise, when making a left turn, to pull off on the road's shoulder, wait for traffic to clear, and then make your turn.

While anyone in Mexico will be happy to give directions, most people have no idea where you're going or how to get you there! Since most Mexicans don't drive, but walk or ride the bus to get from place to place, they have no knowledge of road names or numbers. Also, a vast number of Mexicans never have been outside their native towns, so asking them how to reach a city a hundred miles away would be an impossible task akin to asking how to drive to Thailand.

So, if you have to stop and ask for directions, it is best to do so at a gas station, a hotel, or some other major building. There you will probably find drivers who are accustomed to the roads and may be able to help you. I also find it helpful to carry a pad of paper and a pen with me. I sometimes can't understand Spanish well enough to follow someone's verbal directions, but I usually manage just fine if my helper draws a map.

I mentioned earlier that the Mexican government tries to save money by conserving road signs, and I think they take the same frugal approach when it comes to moderating traffic speed. Rather than install expensive stoplights, they have discovered some very inexpensive solutions to control traffic. In almost every town in Mexico, you will encounter *topes* (TOE-pays) or speed bumps. Some of these are mild-mannered gentle bumps in the road that do no more than warn you politely that you're approaching a town, but others are mountains that bounce your car high into the air and shout that you'd better slow down. After you've hit a *tope* at 40 mph, you will never again approach an urban setting (and bear in mind that an "urban setting" may be a few houses and a couple stores on both sides of a patch of road) without looking for the ubiquitous *topes*. The Mexicans call *topes* sleeping policemen, and I can certainly understand why!

Kilometers Versus Miles

If you are accustomed to driving in the United States, it may be difficult for you to adjust to estimating driving time using kilometers. A rough way to figure miles from kilometers is to multiply the kilometers times 6 and then drop the last digit. A distance of 100 kilometers (100 x 6 = 600), drop the last digit and the distance becomes 60 miles.

Driving at Night – Don't Do It

You've probably already been warned about driving at night in Mexico, and I can't emphasize enough that this is good advice. There are three reasons for this. A truck driver with a flat tire may have stopped on the road earlier in the day and conscientiously placed boulders behind him to direct cars to the other lane while he changed the tire. But when his car was road-worthy again, the chances are that he didn't go back to move those rocks. During the day this is a minor problem, but at night it presents a major hazard.

Another reason is that most ranchers cannot afford to

fence their land, so cows and horses routinely cross major (and minor) roads whenever they like. When the air cools down at night, cows, in particular, seek the heat-absorbing asphalt to stay warm. They love to lie down in the middle of the road and have yet to learn that this is a deadly practice.

The last reason for avoiding night driving is that some Mexican drivers believe they are preserving their car batteries by not turning on their lights at night. If the rocks or the cows in the middle of the road don't get you, the car with no lights will, so please avoid driving after daylight hours!

Buying Gas

When you need to refuel, you will have to use the government maintained Pemex (an acronym for petroleum Mexico) stations. There are no self-service pumps in Mexico. The attendant will ask for the key to your locked tank and fill your car with leaded or unleaded gasoline. *Magna Sin* means without lead--87 octane. *Magna* is premium gas at 93 octane. By the way, diesel fuel is readily available throughout the country. If you want the tank filled, rather than specifying a particular peso amount, just say, "*Lleno,* (pronounced YEAH-no and rhymes with "hey, no.") *por favor.*" If your windows are washed or your tires checked, you may want to give a three or so pesos tip. While most attendants are honest, some people have been short-changed either in gas or in getting their change. Since I like to stretch my legs on a long trip anyway, I try to avoid these problems by getting out of the van and emptying the litter basket while keeping an eye on the gas meter and by counting my change carefully.

Sometimes there are young entrepreneurs hanging around the gas station. These children will try to sell you everything from Chiclets to parakeets. If you want to stop their barrage of buying requests but don't trust your Spanish, simply wave your index finger at them in a "no-no" kind of way. This gesture seems to be accepted throughout Mexico as a polite way of saying "no thank you."

About *Mordidas*

Any guidebook you consult will talk about bribes (*mordidas*) that sometimes are paid to policemen who stop drivers on trumped up charges. Although the government has largely curtailed this practice, a policeman may still try to extort money from you. Remember these points and you should be able to avoid having to pay *mordida*.

When a policeman stops you, even though you've broken no law, he may ask for your driver's license. A favorite way of getting *mordida* is to say he will keep your license until you pay for the "ticket" right then and there. If he asks to see your license, show it to him, but do not let him take it. If he does so anyway, get out your notepad and ask for his name and badge number. (*Su nombre, por favor? Su numero?*) Then get out of your car to walk around and get his license plate number.

This will almost always stop any further action on the policeman's part, and he will return your license and tell you to go on. The reason is because the policeman knows he is doing something illegal (keeping your license) on trumped up charges, and he realizes you're savvy enough to report him. He would rather let you drive on than lose his job.

Sometimes you may have committed an infraction and should receive a ticket, but the policeman will try to extract a bribe rather than give you the standard legitimate fine. This happened to me in October, 2003. My companion ran a red light in Saltillo. He was tired from an eleven-hour drive and was struggling to find the hotel in the dark. Even though the light turned red as we drove through the intersection, we were pulled over almost immediately.

The policeman asked for his driver's license and said the fine was 700 pesos. We would have to pay the next day to get the license back. He undoubtedly knew we were on our way to the States and didn't have an extra day to waste at the courthouse. He was hoping we'd give him the 700 pesos (an exorbitant fee, by the way) to avoid the delay.

I got out of the car, walked around to write down the cruiser's license plate number, and politely asked the officer for his name and badge number. He responded by handing me my friend's driver's license and waving us on.

If you do commit a violation and the policeman does not try to get *mordida*, accept the ticket with good grace, and do not be alarmed by the size of the fine. If you pay within five days, the price is reduced to half the amount written on the ticket. There are also no insurance penalties for tickets, and your driving license is not affected in any way.

If an Accident Occurs

If you're involved in an accident, the first thing to remember is not to panic. You've got copies of all your documents in the glove compartment, you have insurance, and while it may take a while to untangle the details, you will be able to take care of the situation and get underway again.

You may not even need to use your insurance if the accident didn't cause injury or death to anyone involved. In other words, if it's a fender-bender, the police encourage you to work things out with the two drivers reaching an amicable settlement. The police do not need to be called at all in this situation. You can simply hand over the agreed-upon amount of pesos if the accident was your fault, shake hands, and be on your way.

If the accident is more serious, then the police and your insurance adjuster should be called. If you must move your car out of the line of traffic, take pictures first or make a diagram showing what happened. The hardest part of all this is waiting for the adjuster to show up. But, when he/she does, matters will quickly be under control, you'll be told what to do next, and you can be on your way shortly if you can still drive your car. If you need a tow truck, your adjuster will be able to arrange for one.

For further information about what to do when involved in an accident, see this website.

http://www.drivemex.com/Your_Legal_Rights.htm

11 CHOOSING A RENTAL

Since this is written with the frugal expatriate in mind, I assume you're not going to buy a house. If the urge to own property overcomes you, however, please wait at least six months before you make a decision. I know a few people who invested their life savings only to discover their house was in direct line with the sewage treatment plant. They have to keep their windows closed at all times! You really need six months to explore various neighborhoods, decide on village or country life, and to know the area in general before making such a momentous decision. If you know you won't be able to resist buying, please see the section on "Real Estate" for further information.

The easiest way to find a rental is by using the services

of a real estate company. The English speaking realtor will show you a lot of houses, make the transaction easy, and provide back up in case something goes wrong. If you choose to use this approach, make sure you contact many rental agencies. There is no multiple listing service for rentals in Mexico, so it is wise to contact several agencies to see all the options offered in your area.

While an agency may be the easiest approach to house-hunting, it is usually not the cheapest. Here in Ajijic, you must pay the first and last month's rent as well as a security deposit before getting the keys. Then, too, the agency expects you to notify them of needed repairs during your first two weeks of tenancy and then repair bills, except for major ones, come out of your own pocket. Also, remember that 15% of your monthly rent goes to the agency and 85% to the homeowner. You can save that 15% if you rent from the homeowner directly.

In Mexico, word of mouth is often the best way to locate a rental. Ask everyone you meet if he/she knows of a house for rent. Scour the bulletin boards and the newspaper classifieds. Walk through residential areas you like and watch for *"Renta"* signs in the windows. If you're fluent in Spanish, ask painters and plumbers if they know of available rentals. If you are persistent, you will eventually find the place that's right for you.

A Few Words of Caution

If you do not bring a car to Mexico, or if you want to be close to all the action, you will most likely want to live in the village. But there are a few things to keep in mind about village life. Because there are no zoning laws in Mexico, you must choose your location carefully. Is there a "party house" nearby where, when it is rented once a week or so, will blare music until 3:00 in the morning? Are there roosters in the neighbor's backyard to wake you up at 4:00 in the morning? Does the guy across the street have three German shepherds that bark for several hours each day?

To make sure you avoid these problems, take a few precautions. Ask the neighbors. They will most likely be honest since they have nothing to gain by your choice. Drive or walk by the house you'd like to rent at all hours of the day and night to check the noise level. If you can find out who used to live there, give the person a call and ask why he/she moved.

Country Life

If you prefer to live outside the village, you will usually find a quieter life more closely approximating life back in the States, Canada or Europe. There are "gated" communities where a guard makes sure that only tenants or guests are permitted access to the mostly expatriate neighborhoods, and lots of other neighborhoods with a Mexican/expatriate mix. Some of these places are served by the bus system, but others require the use of a car. Once you've decided on either village or country living and found a house, then go on to negotiate a lease with your landlord.

Lease

While only a lease in Spanish can be upheld in a court of law, it is still advantageous to get a lease in both Spanish and English so that you know what you're signing! Most landlords won't mind supplying both.

While you may have to bargain for this, it should also be possible to pay only the first month's rent and a reasonable security deposit of $200-300 US. In Mexico, usually a landlord is also responsible for paying water costs (but not your personal drinking water), neighborhood association (called *colonos*) fees, and the gardener's salary. Typically, your responsibilities will be to pay the electricity and gas bills, television cable or satellite fees, and your maid's salary. Once you and the realtor or landlord have agreed on the terms, you and he/she sign the lease along with two witnesses.

Bear in mind that Mexico does not require realtors to go through the same training and licensing as in the States. While most of them are honest, it is wise to double-check everything the realtor (or landlord) tells you. If you're told the house has a water purification system, ask for instructions on how to change the filters. If there's a satellite system, make sure the "card" is in the box near the TV. If having a phone is important to you, make sure there is already a line, and preferably a telephone, in the house. If there is no telephone, get yours and plug it in. If you don't get a dial tone, you do not have a phone line. It can take anywhere from two months to two years to get a phone line installed and cost around $200. You probably will not want to wait that long or pay that much!

In addition to double-checking the accuracy of the realtor/landlord's information, you will want to make sure you understand the mechanics of the house.

Here are some important questions to ask:

What kind of **gas** container do I have? If you have a tank on the roof, you will need to call the company when it needs re-filling. If you have portable gas cylinders, you will put a sign on your gate to notify the men as they pass by that you need replacements.

Do I have a *tinaco* (a tank on the roof that dispenses water through your pipes using gravity) or a **water pump**? If you have a water pump, you may need to prime it after a power outage. It's better to learn how to do that now, rather than at midnight some rainy night.

Where is the **fuse box?** In one of my houses, I kept blowing the fuse when I forgot that the washing machine and dishwasher could not operate simultaneously.

Where is the **water heater**? Most water heaters are located outside and the wind can frequently blow out the flame. Learn how to re-light the pilot, or, better yet, find a way to protect the flame from the wind.

Can paper be flushed down the **toilet?** In many of the village houses, built long, long ago, the sewer pipes are very narrow and cannot accommodate toilet paper.

With some plumbing systems, it is necessary to put the paper in the wastebasket. In newer homes, or renovated village homes with improved plumbing, the paper can go right down the drain with no problem.

Do I **pay rent** in pesos or US dollars? Will you accept a check? It is sometimes much easier to write a check than to make several trips to the ATM machine or to stand in line at Lloyd's.

Do you mind if I make **improvements** to the property? In Mexico, you can do almost anything you like to a house--from painting the walls red to installing extra mirrors—and the landlord will not mind. Still, it's better to get permission beforehand.

Do not forget to get a receipt every time you pay rent. You may need proof of residency when applying for visa renewals, so the receipts are important.

Remember, too, that if you believe you've been treated unfairly by a Mexican individual or business, you can contact the *Procuraduria Federal del Consumidor,* known to most everyone by its acronym Profeco. It's the equivalent of the Better Business Bureau in the States and is the best protection consumers have against fraud. They are there to

intercede on your behalf. The Spanish website is
http://www.profeco.gob.mx

Scorpions

While you might dislike the thought of living in a country with scorpions, they are nothing to fear if you take a few precautions.

Before you move into your house, have it fumigated and fumigate thereafter every three months or so. You can hire someone to do this for about 300 pesos, or you can do it yourself for 30 pesos.   The do-it-yourself method involves buying a hand-held refillable spray canister and a product called Cyn-Off from any local hardware store.   Mix the Cyn-Off with water according to the directions and spray the perimeter of the outside of your house and all the inside perimeter floor edges.   Be sure to pay close attention to dark areas in closets, under the stove, and behind the refrigerator. When your maid mops the floor, be sure she includes a detergent that expels bugs in addition to any other cleaning agent.

Scorpions are nocturnal creatures that go about looking for bugs by night and curl up in soft, warm places to sleep by day.   If you see one during the day, it is probably sick and sluggish. You will be able to kill it quickly with the slap of a shoe. When darkness falls, be sure to close any doors leading to your terrace. To avoid stepping on one during nighttime bathroom visits, keep a pair of rubber thongs or flip flops by the bed. In the morning, shake out your clothes and shoes—just in case.

If you are stung, although most of the time it's no more serious than a bee sting, it is still wise to have a decongestant on hand and a soothing ointment or salve. If you are one of the few who is allergic and you begin to have a reaction, seek medical attention immediately.

In four years of living in Mexico, I've killed about a dozen scorpions. Not a single one has gotten me yet!

My Renting History

My first two and a half years in Mexico were spent in a lovely house in a development on the outskirts of Ajijic. I had two bedrooms and two baths, an office with built-in bookshelves and desk, a large living/dining/kitchen combination, a covered terrace and a walled garden and *mirador*. (A *mirador* literally means view, but, in Mexico, it's also used to refer to a panoramic rooftop area reached by an outside staircase.) The house was beautifully furnished and rented for $550 a month. After the first year, I was able to convince the Mexican landlords to collect my rent themselves and avoid the realty company. That dropped my rent to $500.

I eventually decided to try village life, though, and moved to a huge property close to the lakefront and just one block from the main business district. The "estate," as my friends called it, was located on a lovely ¾ acre of ground with mature fruit trees and a large swimming pool. There were two buildings on the property—a *casita* consisting of two levels, each with its own entrance, bedroom and bathroom and my house which had three levels—living room on the first floor, kitchen/family room on the second, and bedroom on the third. I rented the *casita* for $300 a month which brought my rent down to an almost unbelievable $200 a month.

But that house was anything but paradise. The grapefruit trees produced fifty fruit a day so I spent one hour daily for two months picking them up. And I hate grapefruit! The pool was, as my Mexican landlord said, problematic, so it might be green one month and blue the next. One of the hotels behind me sponsored live music every weekend so I could sleep only if I used earplugs every Friday, Saturday, and Sunday night. My neighbor, who was deaf, had a dog that loved to bark for hours and hours every day, and the weavers on the lakefront, thinking they were providing community service, burned any trash they found so smoke overwhelmed my house several times a day. I also found my exorbitant utility bills negated any advantage I thought I was getting from my low rent. Needless to say, I left that place as soon as I found someone willing to take over my lease. By the way, the new tenant is quite happy there. He says his hearing was damaged in Viet Nam so he doesn't notice the noise, he can't wait to eat the grapefruit, and he likes to clean his own pool.

My last house is also in the village but in a very quiet part of town. It is a very old structure, mostly adobe with 16-inch thick walls and three fireplaces, built in the hacienda style. I have two bedrooms separated by a bathroom on one side of the terrace and a living room, kitchen and dining area on the other side. Beyond the kitchen are another spacious living room, another bathroom, and a staircase leading to a third bedroom and private balcony overlooking the lake and the mountains. With a rent of $400 a month and very low utility bills, I plan to live here for the next twenty years!

By the way, one of the reasons it's relatively easy to move when you're dissatisfied is because local moving men will transport your belongings, or even pack for you, for very little money. In Ajijic, Augustin Sanchez packed my things one day and spent six hours the next day moving my furniture from the three-level "mansion" for 1250 pesos. He moved me another time for just 1000 pesos. Needless to say, I always give him a substantial tip.

Sample Rental Prices in Ajijic, June, 2010

While David and I were in Ajijic the summer of 2010, our friends, Gloria and Heinz, moved into a newly constructed house in the village. Their house has a spacious front terrace and a back patio with a garden. Inside, the first floor consists of a huge living room/dining room combination, a beautiful kitchen I envied, a bedroom and full bath. Upstairs there was a large TV/study area the same size as the downstairs living area, two more bedrooms and a full bath. All this was theirs for $650 a month!

Here are some ads I noticed on the Lake Chapala

Society bulletin board this summer. There's a two-bedroom, one and a half bath furnished aChapterment that includes electricity and maid service just three blocks from the lake for $300 US.

If two bedrooms aren't necessary, you could rent a one-bedroom casita with a fireplace, screened porch, garden and gardener that's within walking distance to shopping for $450 US.

Or how about a furnished one-bedroom casita with two terraces, DSL Internet, electric, incredible views, and a pool just one block from the plaza for $500 US?

If you simply want to try a short-term rental before making a commitment, you can lease—until October—this upper Ajijic house with two bedrooms, two baths, a patio and garden, maid, phone, and Internet service for $500 US.

If you're sure this is the place you want to be, however, there's a long-term rental for $850 US that includes 2000 square feet in a two-story house with two bedrooms and two baths, washer/dryer, and patio.

Other Options

There are a few ways to live in Mexico and pay reduced or no rent, but you will probably have to live here a while before you can use one of these ideas. After you get to know the community, though, and have found some reliable service people, you can take advantage of the demographics in most expatriate communities. Most towns are full of retirees who travel a great deal or who return to their native countries for a good part of the year, so it is possible to arrange situations that benefit both you and the retiree.

Several people house and/or pet sit. Here in Ajijic the going rate for house sitting is 100 pesos per day, and if there are pets involved, the fee is 120 pesos. Some couples maintain a home but offset their rental costs by the husband's spending several nights a month at whatever home they've promised to watch. Other house sitters do not charge because they do not maintain a house. They simply go from job to job, staying with friends if there's an off day or two. My friend Karen stays in the most luxurious houses, almost always with a pool and spa, and has yet to pay a centavo for rent. Because she is honest, conscientious, and loves animals, she is in high demand and is asked to sit for more houses than she can handle.

Another idea to lower rental costs is to "share" a house with someone. Many people own homes that they occupy only one or two months a year. It is sometimes possible to rent one of these houses if you are willing to vacate the house for the month(s) the owners will be in residence. You can plan your own vacation around the time of the owners' visit, and, because you do not pay rent or utilities during the time the owners are there, that lowers your overall rent considerably.

Yet a third option is to rent a *casita* (a little house) that's Chapter of a much larger property. You can be the caretaker for the Big House and tend to any problems that arise in return for decreased rent. In most cases, the owners will only be on the property for a few months a year.

Buying Real Estate

In the United States and Canada, there are many advantages to owning your own home. Not only can the interest be written off on taxes, but home ownership can be a hedge against inflation, and a hefty profit can be realized when the house has appreciated in value.

The same rules do not apply in Mexico. Lending institutions do not grant mortgages. The likely scenario is that you will have to pay cash for the house. You will not have any interest to deduct from your taxes, and you will not be earning interest or dividends on the capital you could have invested elsewhere. Owning a house does not necessarily protect you from inflation either. In Mexico, a country where inflation is rampant, property values fall with the economy rather than rise. In other words, if the peso plummets, a highly likely occurrence, then so does your real estate value.

But what if you have your heart set on restoring some colonial gem? At the risk of contradicting what I've just said, if the joys of restoring a house can overcome all the drawbacks to property ownership, then go right ahead. Actually, a friend of mine bought a village house in 2002 for under $50,000, spent ten months happily covering the walls with a rainbow of different colors and doing minor repairs, and sold it a year later for a $19,000 profit. It can be done. But it doesn't happen very often.

Another friend, who has a master's degree in real

estate from the US and who beautifully renovated her own village home, suggests that you carefully inspect any house you are considering for restoration. Make sure the roof doesn't leak, that the toilets flush, and that rebar serves as the structural support behind the walls. It is a very good idea to hire a structural (civil) engineer to make an inspection before you make a commitment.

12 SETTLING IN

Many times the gardener is included in your rent so you usually do not have to worry about this. If you need to find your own, however, check the bulletin boards, ask your neighbors if their gardeners have any extra time, or walk around the village, knock on the doors of people whose gardens you admire, and ask them how to contact the grounds keeper. Typically, a grounds keeper takes care of your property for two to four hours a couple days a week and earns about 50 pesos per hour. They are also handymen who can change light bulbs in hard to reach fixtures, help you carry in the groceries, and repair most anything in your house.

A maid can be located in much the same way. Oftentimes a realtor will suggest a particular maid, but it is unwise to accept the choice since the housekeeper's loyalty will be to the realtor rather than to you. So, once again, ask your neighbors and check the bulletin boards but also look at the classifieds.

Many people try to help their housekeepers find extra work and will take the trouble to place an ad. These maids are usually highly reliable and good, honest workers.

How to Instruct Your Maid

Since having a housekeeper may be one of your new luxuries in Mexico, it may take a while for you to become comfortable with having someone else in your house. But try to adjust because you will soon find her indispensable!

Housekeeping in Mexico is a respectable job, and, because there are many benefits to this type of employment, you will find your maid to be a congenial and resourceful worker. When she arrives at your home, she should be shown a room where she can put her belongings and be allowed to change clothes, if necessary. During the work period, she should be allowed some short breaks, and it's a nice gesture to offer a soda. If she has had to take a bus to get to your house, offer to pay the three or four peso bus fare for the return trip.

While **part-time** employees are not entitled by law to a Christmas bonus, it is a goodwill gesture to do so.

Generally the bonus should be the equivalent of two weeks' pay. So, if your maid works four hours a week for 160 pesos, then you will give her a 320 peso bonus before December 15, in addition to her usual 160 pesos for that week.

On Mexican holidays, the law requires that your **full-time** maid be given the day off with pay, or given double pay if she works that day. The official Mexican holidays are: January 1, New Year's Day; February 5, Constitution Day; March 21, Benito Juarez Day; May 1, Labor Day; September 16, Independence Day; November 20, Revolution Day and December 25, Christmas Day. It is also a very good idea to keep a written record of all payments made and to have your housekeeper sign that record as acknowledgment.

Some people hire maids on a full-time basis, but I think that's unnecessary. Having her come once a week for four hours or twice a week for two or three hours should suffice. You will also have to tell your housekeeper exactly what you want her to do. Pantomime works well if your Spanish isn't up to par, and working with her the first time or two is a good idea also. Don't be surprised if your maid does not know how to operate a vacuum cleaner on your rugs. Most floors in Mexico are tile and no vacuuming is required. Simply demonstrate how to turn on the machine and how to use it; she'll soon catch on.

One word of warning is needed here. Since most maids have never used a computer and have no idea how delicate they are, it is wise to make sure your maid will not disconnect the computer cord in order to plug in the vacuum cleaner. Either put tape over the plug you don't want disconnected, or tell her in no uncertain terms that it should never be dislodged.

This is what my housekeeper does each week during a four-hour period for 160 pesos. She sweeps and mops all the tile floors and terrace, vacuums the rugs, cleans the bathrooms, dusts the furniture, changes the bed sheets, and washes the dishes. This is a reasonable workload for the time period, but if you'd prefer to have your maid iron clothes, or cook lunch, substitute that for one of the other items.

Mexican workers make do with the simplest items, but you should have these things on hand to make sure your house is cleaned properly. A broom is the most essential tool. You will also need a mop, one with long strands, that can be wrung out—American sponge mops don't last long on tile floors. Also buy a large bucket that has a "wringing out" plastic device on one end. Have lots of old rags or whatever you prefer to use for dusting. You'll also need a toilet brush and a scrubbing brush for bathroom cleaning.

The cleaning supplies are a bit different in Mexico. You will need a product called Fabulosa, available at any grocery or drugstore, to keep the tile floors looking shiny and Ajax Expel to encourage bugs and scorpions to stay outside instead of visiting your house. For some reason I have yet to understand, Mexican housekeepers love window cleaner and use it by the gallon. You can't buy too much. You will also need the usual disinfecting type of liquid cleanser and perhaps, if you have stained toilets, a product called Sultana. Sultana is muriatic acid, and, while it's probably outlawed in other countries, it removes stains from porcelain better than anything I've ever seen. If you use Sultana, be sure to have protective rubber gloves for your housekeeper as well as a pumice stone for the removal of persistent stains.

A Few Precautions

Stringent laws protect Mexican domestic workers, and most of them are fully familiar with their rights. If your housekeeper does not perform satisfactorily, or if you are displeased with her for any reason, you must fire her within the first thirty days. During this time period you can terminate her employment without giving a reason. If you keep her on longer than that, you will have to pay her severance. Since severance pay is calculated according to a complicated formula, and even realtors engage lawyers to arrive at the exact figure, try to avoid ever getting in this situation.

Some people give the maid the key to the house and others always make sure they're home when the housekeeper is working. Most maids are honest and hardworking, but there's a small minority who steal. Police often report that burglaries seem to be "inside" jobs because there's no sign of forced entry, and the maid is frequently suspect. You will have to decide what is comfortable for you, but it's probably a good idea to wait at least a little while, perhaps a month, before handing over a key.

Cost-of-Living

The low cost-of-living is one of the main attractions of Mexico, of course, but you will get a different response as to the actual costs from anyone you ask. I recently read a book written in the mid-80's that promised a wonderful lifestyle on $250 a month. Howells and Merwin's *Choose Mexico for Retirement,* published in

1999, suggests a budget of $600 a month. A poll of all my friends suggests that anywhere from $800-1500 was a more reasonable figure for the Ajijic area in 2003. In 2010, a friend who has lived in Ajijic for twelve years said that a homeowner can live comfortably on $1200 while a renter needs between $1500-1700 US.

But, of course, as my friend Kurt pointed out, only you know what is essential to your comfort. If you want to eat in restaurants every day rather than shop at the market, your bills will be higher.

Internet Sites for Cost-of-Living

<u>http://www.rollybrook.com/cost_of_living.htm</u>
Rolly's costs in Lerdo, Durango, Mexico

http://www.chapala.com/chapala/cost.html Provides figures on cost-of-living in Ajijic. Please note, though, that a few categories on this page do not match my recent experiences. I recently paid $33 US for teeth cleaning, and had a cavity repaired for $40. Also, since electricity costs have continued to rise, I think the figure on this page should be doubled.

http://www.mexscape.net/Shopping/living-cheap-the-cost-of-things-in-mazatlan.html

See this website for thoughts on the cost the Mazatlan beach community.

Internet Sites for Rentals

In the Ajijic/Lake Chapala region:

http://www.lagunamex.com This is one of the largest rental companies in town.

http://www.eagerrealty.com/rentals.html   More expensive properties are listed on this site.

In San Miguel de Allende:

http://www.san-miguel-house-rentals.com/ Lists very expensive vacation rentals.

These sites lists apartments and houses for short and long-term rentals.

http://www.sanmiguelrentals.com/property.html

http://portalsanmiguel.com/real-estate/for-rent/

In Guadalajara:

http://www.allaboutguadalajara.com/ While this site does not list many specific houses for rent, it does supply contact information for local realtors.

In Oaxaca:

http://bestofoaxaca.com/ This site lists houses, provides pictures, and supplies lots of details.

There are many more real estate agencies in Oaxaca, but they do not have websites. If interested in this region, try calling one of these agencies when you're in the city:

Contacto Inmobiliario - 513-2672
Construcciones y Diseños AM - 520-0485
Residencial Puente de Piedra - 518-4286
Pliego Inmobiliaria - 513-3010
Century 21 - 516-0323

13 WAYS TO SAVE MONEY

As is the case in any country, there are ways to save money that are relatively painless. If you follow this advice in Mexico, you will save several hundreds of dollars per month.

The Mail

If you can possibly arrange for a Mexican post office box before you move, that is the wisest course of action. If you haven't done this ahead of time, be sure to make it one of your first priorities after arrival.

While some people assume the government mail system will be unreliable, I have only "lost" two things over the past three years, a record comparable to my experience in the States. In general, while the mail may take three to six weeks to reach you, it is generally trustworthy.

There are two other advantages to having a post office box. The fee of one peso per month is far more reasonable than the 250-300 pesos per month charged by a commercial mail service. A Mexican post office box is also the only way to avoid having to pay hefty fees for customs. This is very important. Because my insurance pays for prescription drugs in the States, for four years my sister regularly mailed my drugs to my post office box. They always arrived in a timely fashion. (By the way, it is perfectly legal to send prescription drugs through the mail.) If, on the other hand, she had sent them via a mail service, they either would never arrive at all or be held at customs for a $30-50 additional fee. This same practice applies to any other item sent from the States whether it is a book or a pair of jeans –a commercial mail service must send the item through customs and there will always be additional fees, if you ever receive it at all!

I'll never forget the day I was standing in a local Mexican Mailboxes Etc. listening to a woman sob as she explained her story to the clerk. This woman had returned to the States for medical treatment, the doctors had discovered cancer, they'd put her on an aggressive drug regimen and then allowed her to return to Mexico since she couldn't afford to stay in the States for treatment. She had the drugs shipped via Mailboxes because she thought a commercial mail service was the only way to safely ensure their arrival, but now she could not receive them at all. They'd been detained at customs, the clerk explained, and probably would never be allowed to cross the border.

So, I believe most expatriates will want a post office box, but if you're unable to obtain one before you move and need a temporary forwarding address, you may want to contract with a commercial mail service for a few months. The website for Mailboxes Etc. is http://www.mbe.com

Food

The best source of **fresh produce** is the weekly market, or *tianguis*. Every town in Mexico has one and the prices are the lowest to be found locally. David and I bought quart-size containers of red raspberries, blackberries and strawberries—the best we've ever tasted—the summer of 2010 for 25 pesos ($2) each. Because a lot of the produce is grown organically in someone's small garden and brought to the market at the peak of freshness, you will find that fruits and vegetables in Mexico taste better than anywhere else in the world. Going to the market is always a pleasant experience too, because you run into friends and the shopping trip becomes a social event.

By the way, you will find a lot of things besides fruits and vegetables at the market. This is where I routinely buy a bouquet of roses or mixed flowers for 25 pesos, plastic items for the kitchen at below-store price, CDs at below-market price (The copyright laws in Mexico are few and seldom enforced.) and electronic goods. When I needed a lamp wired, the local hardware store quoted a 90 pesos estimate, but the local market electrician did the job for 30 pesos. I always take visitors to the market, too, and they report it's one of the high points of the vacation.

If you can't get to the weekly *tianguis*, you will always find fresh produce at the town's permanent market. Often called the *mercado*, it's usually located near a plaza side street. While smaller in scale, it carries a lot of the same things you find at the weekly market plus a few extras like baked goods and rotisserie chicken. At Chapala's *mercado*, the most mouth-watering whole chicken, oven-roasted potatoes, and rice/vegetable medley can be had for fewer than 80 pesos. It's enough for two people and you'll undoubtedly have leftovers for another meal or two.

In Guadalajara, and in most other large cities, there is an *abastos*, or market section, which serves vendors in a fifty-mile radius. Although it is designed to serve primarily wholesale buyers, you can buy smaller quantities of food at very low prices. My *abastos* stretches for twenty blocks. Here you will find dozens of short side streets where vendors specialize in just one kind of produce. For example, there's one block devoted to nothing but tomatoes and another carries only chilies. There, too, you will see stores like Mama's where huge bins hold thirty pounds of sugar, flour, spices, nuts, candy and herbs. A helpful attendant will scoop out what you need into a plastic bag.

Don't forget that fresh produce grown in Mexico requires special handling. Because it's organically grown, any fruits or vegetables that cannot be peeled must be soaked in a solution made from tap water and a product called Microdyne or Albiosan. You can find this for fewer than 10 pesos at any grocery store. Simply soak your produce in a bowl with five drops of Microdyne per liter of tap water for fifteen minutes before you eat it.

Get your **fresh bread and rolls** at your local *panaderia*. Usually hidden on a side street, it's well worth looking for, so ask your neighbors or watch for the pan sign. Here you will find *bolillos*, delicious crusty sandwich or dinner rolls, and huge, gooey cinnamon rolls for just a few pesos. My local *panaderia* also sells raw dough that can be turned into pizza or pastry that can be used for pies.

For **staples** and other food items, including **meats and poultry**, locate your closest *Mega Mercado*, Wal-Mart, Sam's Club or Costco. Although there is now a Wal-Mart in Ajijic and one in San Miguel de Allende (it goes by a different name, but it is a Wal-Mart) people in the Lake Chapala region still make this shopping excursion to Costco at least once a month, if not weekly. In Guadalajara, the Wal-Mart, Sam's Club and Costco are clustered in the same area, so it's easy to get everything you need very quickly. By the way, I would strongly suggest you take a cooler with you for your perishable items.

As is true with produce in Mexico, you will find that the range-fed pork and poultry are much better than anything you've eaten before. Chicken is a more natural color, rather than the artificial yellow you find in Canada and the US; and the pork, from pigs that are allowed to roam free and are often treated like pets on family farms, is incredibly good. Unfortunately, the same practices do not result in the tender beef we're used to back home. It is unusual to find aged beef, and you must marinate or slow-cook most beef to produce a tender cut.

Other Items

You can certainly find **cleaning supplies** in any store in Mexico, but the cheapest prices are found at neighborhood *Limpieza* Total stores. The one around the corner from my house has shelves lined with plastic bottles in all shapes and sizes holding bleach, laundry detergent for white clothes and special detergent with a little bit of dye in it for dark clothes, and *Fabulosa* for tile floors.

Remember that there are no super stores, such as Home Depot, in the smaller Mexican towns although you will find them in large cities. **Building supplies** are purchased at stores specializing in just one product such as wood (*carpinteria*) or glass (*vidrios*). When thinking about home improvement, don't forget the *herrerias*, metal workers. They craft some magnificent items from bed headboards to coffee tables at prices that are often cheaper than the same product would cost in wood.

The *herrerias* are also able to reproduce almost any

item you can imagine if shown a picture and given dimensions. I once took a catalog from an exclusive and expensive store in the States to Manuel, showed him the $46 US towel rack I admired, and he duplicated it for 60 pesos.

Utilities

Your utility bills must be paid promptly in Mexico, or you risk disconnection and a service fee to get things running again. Even if you have a post office box, these bills will be delivered to the actual street address. If you are going to be out of town for a long vacation, be sure to have a friend pay these bills or, if you have an account there, use Lloyd's bill-paying service.

The **telephone** is a monopoly run by a company called Telmex (An acronym for telephone and Mexico.). While the telephones and the seven digit numbers will be familiar to you, here you will find a different billing system. Unlike most of North America where a set monthly fee entitles you to unlimited phone calls, in Mexico you receive only 100 phone calls for the monthly fee, and every phone call after that entails an extra charge of 1.48 pesos.

monthly rate is relatively low, around 185 pesos, it is all too easy to run up an expensive bill in no time. That's because your basic service provides for only those 100 calls per month, which amounts to approximately three calls per day per month. If you access the computer via dial-up only twice a day, that's two "phone calls" because you are using the telephone modem. That means you can only make one other phone call per day, or you will exceed your three-calls-a-day maximum.

Try these tips to keep your budget in line. Limit the number of times you use the Internet, or get wireless Internet. Rather than call your friends, send them e-mails. You can send a dozen messages for the price of one modem phone call. When someone gives you a cell phone number, tell him you'd prefer to have his regular at-home phone number. Do not dial cell phone numbers unless there's no other choice.

As for calls to other countries, it is imperative to have a callback service. Most expatriate communities in Mexico have such services, and you can find one that's right for you by checking the newspaper or asking friends. My callback service (I dial a number, hang up, then, when the phone rings, dial the number in the States.) requires no monthly fee, bills in six-second increments, costs 21 cents per minute, and sends an accounting to my e-mail address every month. My credit card is charged only for the calls I actually make.

Another alternative, if you have the proper computer set up, is to use a Voice over Internet Protocol (VoIP) such as Vonage or Skype. What you need is a computer with an audio card that has both a speaker and a microphone plug, a set of headphones, a microphone, and a VoIP telephone provider. Through the magic of digital technology, the telephone number entered on your computer screen is routed to a telephone modem in the US or Canada. You use your headset just as you would a telephone. Depending on the package you choose, you will pay about 3.5 cents per minute to calls in the States and 4.3 cents to Canada. See this website for further information and calling plans. http://www.iconnecthere.com

Also, bear in mind that local phone bills are always one month behind. If you move into your house in September, the first bill you receive at the end of the month will be for August. Obviously your landlord should pay that bill out of the previous tenant's security deposit. Conversely, when you move, you will be responsible for the last month's telephone bill which will not be delivered until a month later.

One other point to remember is that the telephone will be kept in the landlord's name. If your bill does not arrive in a timely fashion or gets lost (Since mine was simply thrown in my driveway, this sometimes happened.) you may have to go to the Telmex office to ask for a copy. While the clerk can usually access the bill using the telephone number, it would be helpful also to have the name that's listed on the account.

Electricity is very expensive in Mexico. Try, if possible, to use only energy-saving appliances and limit the number of lights you leave on or change the bulbs to fluorescent ones; if you have a dishwasher, use it only when it's completely full; and never use an electric dryer.

In most parts of Mexico, the electricity is billed every two months. Here in Ajijic/Chapala, there are local bill-paying stations that are set up for a week or so in convenient locations so that people can avoid having to stand in line at the electric company. It feels a bit peculiar to stand in a clinic to pay your electric bill, but it's far easier than waiting in line for an hour at the electric company! Ask your neighbors where and when you should pay this bill.

Electric bills for two-bedroom houses generally run

around 600-1200 pesos for the two-month period. If you think the bill is too high, ask the electric company to come out and check your wires. If they find nothing amiss, it might be worth your while to hire an electrician to check your inside wiring. A "leak" can cost you hundreds of extra dollars, so it's wise to get it repaired as quickly as possible.

Propane is relatively inexpensive, but the frugal expatriate will still want to be conservative. The single greatest user of propane is the gas dryer. If I were you, to save money, I'd hang my clothes outside. Invest 30 pesos in some clothesline and save five times that sum each month in propane costs. You'll find that your clothes will dry in no time in this land of almost perpetual sunshine and have that wonderful outdoor smell, too.

Another money-saving idea is to turn down the water heater after your morning shower. Your tank will hold enough hot water for each day's dish washing use, and you can turn up the dial the next morning twenty minutes before you want to shower again.

Remember that utility bills must be paid in a timely fashion, or you will pay a hefty reconnection fee. If you are a chronic procrastinator, Lloyd's financial institution will pay the bills out of your account for a modest fee.

Drinking Water

Unless you live in a house with a purification system, you will need to purchase your drinking water. These five-gallon plastic containers are delivered to your door from a truck that drives by your house once or twice a day – just listen for the man calling *"agua"* or put a sign up on your gate or front door. While the cost is fairly small, in Ajijic it's twenty pesos and I give a one peso tip, if you live in the country or want to save money, try to locate a do-it-yourself place. These are becoming more and more popular because the cost is less than half the cost of delivered water. Ajijic is served by three businesses: one in the neighboring town of Chapala, one on the west side of Ajijic, and one in the village of San Antonio. Simply take your empty five-gallon jug to the store where the employees will sanitize it and refill it with purified water for only six pesos.

14 INSURANCE COSTS

Medical Costs and Health Insurance

These are always a concern to anyone moving to another country. Even if you have insurance in your home country, it may not be applicable everywhere in Mexico even though a few hospitals in the larger cities accept US insurance. It would be wise to call your insurance company before you move and find out about your coverage limitations, if any. Bear in mind, too, that, while many people are working to change this, at the present time Medicare is not applicable in Mexico.

You may find you have a situation like mine. My insurance, provided by the state and maintained by Blue Cross at no cost to me as part of my retirement package, covers any sickness or accident costs in any country in the world. While that sounds wonderful, the reality is that there's so much paperwork involved in being reimbursed for most expenses that I don't bother to file claims unless I experience major difficulties. Instead, I prefer to pay for routine care, such as flu shots, out of my own pocket; have my yearly check-ups when I return to the States for vacations; and return to the States if I find I need major surgery or treatment.

If you do not have such an insurance plan, there are several other solutions, all of them roughly 40 to 60% less than comparable insurance plans in the US. Most expatriate associations, such as the Lake Chapala Society, provide information about insurance coverage. Although the association in Ajijic does not sponsor any company, representatives are available once a week for questions.

Bupa from the TioCorp Insurance Brokers, specializes in the Latin American market, but you can find Bupa doctors anywhere in the world. According to their literature, the company has been in business since 1947 and insures more than ten million people from 192 countries around the world. Bupa offers six plans with varying levels of service. You choose which tier of service coverage you prefer and pay the corresponding premium.

In 2010, the least expensive Bupa plan, "Critical Care," with a $2000 annual deduction and a premium, for people over 50, of $1227 annually, is quite popular, according to Ajijic representative Valerie Friesen. Since doctor visits in Mexico are quite reasonable and rarely cost more than $15-25 (equal to the co-pay amount for many insurance plans in the United States), many expats feel comfortable paying for their routine care out of pocket and reserving their Bupa insurance for catastrophic injuries or illnesses.

If more services are required, Bupa offers five other plans with a variety of coverage, including a provision for air lift service to the United States. The company operates similarly to an HMO because, no matter what plan you select, you must first visit a local doctor for a referral to a Bupa specialist. For more information, visit the website at

http://www.bupalatinamerica.com or e-mail Valerie valerie.friesen@tiocorpinc.com

Another company, Seguros Monterrey, was in business for 65 years before partnering with New York Life. **The Seguros Monterrey-New York Life** insurance provides unlimited coverage, with a 10% co-pay, and a range of deductible options.

Unfortunately the website, www.monterrey-newyorklife.com.mx, is in Spanish, so you might find it necessary to talk to a bilingual representative for answers to your questions. In the Ajijic area, Edgar Cadenas, fulfills this role. He is at his Lake Chapala Society office every Tuesday from 11:00 until 2:00. Telephone: (33) 3630-3406

Cell: (33) 3106-6982 E-mail: mexicoprotect@hotmail.com

Catastrophic events are covered, with care offered in either Mexico or the United States, up to $50,000 with only a $50 deductible. Accidents have no deductible.

In case of illness, Seguros Monterrey-New York Life provides your local doctor with a list of approved specialists from which to choose. Note, however, that pre-existing conditions are never covered by this insurance company.

Here is a chart that shows the options available to a hypothetical 62-year-old expatriate. All figures are in pesos.

Deductible	Annual Premium
2400 pesos	26764 pesos
30,000	24247
38,500	22545
55,000	22322

If the insurance company you choose does not have an air evacuation service, or if that is the only option you feel you need, you might consider **SkyMed**. http://www.skymed.com This company, in business since 1989, provides emergency airlift service to members in Canada, Mexico, the Caribbean, Bahamas, Bermuda, Costa Rica, Belize and the United States.

The basic annual premium of $222 buys transport back

to your home or home hospital (Not the closest hospital—an important distinction if the closest hospital is in Texas but your family and friends are in New Hampshire and New Hampshire is where you want medical care.) for you and a cohabiting partner. There is a range of other options, from the basic plan to one that will transport your vehicle and pets back home, with, of course, a range of annual premiums.

Unlike standard insurance policies, this company will provide services for pre-existing conditions after a 90-day waiting period.

If you are wondering if your insurance policy from your home country is viable in other parts of the world, a company called **MD Abroad** (no Internet presence) offers an evaluation service at the Lake Chapala Society during the months of September-April.

Canadians often solve the whole insurance problem by being only part-time residents of Mexico. They arrive at the beginning of the cold season, enjoy Mexico's temperate winters, and return to Canada for the other six months of the year so their health benefits remain intact.

But if you are not Canadian or if none of the

companies suggested by the expatriate association solves your problem or if they are too expensive, you may want to consider the **Instituto Mexicano del Seguro Social (IMSS)** program. This is a national health insurance program available to anyone regardless of age—Mexican and expatriate—similar to Health Maintenance Organizations (HMOs) back in the United States or the national health provided in Canada. You will need a professional's help in navigating the paperwork the first time, but, after you're enrolled, you are eligible for free doctor visits, lab tests, drugs, and surgical procedures. Note that there is a two-year waiting period for pre-existing conditions.

To apply for IMSS, you must provide your birth certificate which has been translated into Spanish; your proof of residence (Use an electric bill or phone bill.); a copy of your passport photo page; a copy of your residence visa; and four passport-size photos. It is helpful to hire a bilingual professional to help you with the paperwork, and Monica Munoz is one of the experts in the Ajijic region. Telephone: (33) 3854-3596 Cell: (33) 1109-5985 E-mail: monicatomica@hotmail.com

In 2010, the annual premium for people 40-59 years old is 2,210.10 pesos (approximately $177 at 12.5

pesos to the dollar) plus a 600 peso ($48) administrative fee. The annual premium for people in the 60-plus age category is 3,325.70 pesos (approximately $266) plus a 600 peso administrative fee. (You may want to consult this web page for more information http://www.focusonmexico.com/Applying_for_IMSS.html).

These extraordinarily low premiums are attractive, but there are a few drawbacks to IMSS. Since most of their doctors and personnel are not bilingual, a patient must pay for a translator to accompany him to doctor appointments. If a specialist is required, it may take from four to eight months to get an appointment. Then, too, while there are many excellent doctors in this program, you are not able to choose the one to whom you'll be assigned. Yours may be the best doctor in town or the worst. Still, even with these limitations, the government sponsored insurance is extremely popular with expatriates because of the generally excellent care and the low rates.

Besides offering excellent care, the IMSS is becoming particularly good at preventive medicine; immunizations and inoculations are now routine. But if you have a serious problem, your local clinic will give you a referral to a hospital in a larger city. For example, after she received a referral from a local doctor, one of my Ajijic friends recently had a cataract removed and a lens implanted in a Guadalajara hospital. She was quite pleased with the medical care.

The summer of 2010, I was introduced to Tony who spent nine days at an IMSS (the national health insurance) hospital at no charge. He will return in two weeks for a quadruple by-pass, and his only "fee" is to find nine volunteers with his rare blood type to donate blood. This blood will replace what the doctors expect to use during Tony's heart surgery.

This blood donation requirement is true for IMSS or "regular" patients who do not have insurance and pay full price for their surgeries. For some reason, nationwide blood drives are unknown in Mexico, so blood is always in short supply. Often you can "bank" your own blood before surgery, or you can usually find volunteers to contribute.

Some people prefer to pay for everything out of pocket. They want to be able to choose their own doctors and hospitals, and they find medical costs quite reasonable. Costs are low because Mexico is not a litigious country and doctors do not need to pay for malpractice insurance. This savings is passed on to the patient. A doctor visit in Ajijic runs around 150 pesos and a specialist visit with an EKG test in Guadalajara costs about 400 pesos, so this is a viable alternative. If you are in reasonably good health, your yearly medical costs may not exceed the deductible for a standard United States insurance plan.

When I developed stomach problems the summer David and I were living in Ajijic for a month, a blood test and doctor visit (total cost $24) revealed typhus. My insurance co-pay for a doctor visit alone in the United States would have exceeded that amount and blood work would have added considerably more to my bill.

Even if you require major surgery, the hospital bills will be considerably less than in the US. A friend of mine, in 2002, had part of her pancreas removed and biopsies of six major organs in a seven-hour operation. She was in intensive care for three days and had private round-the-clock nurses when she was moved to her private room. The total cost for the surgeon, medical supplies, nursing, and hospital room was $15,000.

While David and I were in Mexico, several uninsured

friends told us of their recent pleasant experiences in Guadalajara's private hospitals. The following examples are the total cost (doctor, hospital, nursing) for the procedure or operation. Gordon had an angiogram and spent the night in the hospital for observation—his total bill was $2,000. Joseph had fairly complicated back surgery and spent two nights in a beautiful hospital room for $12,000. Charlotte had a total emergency hysterectomy and was hospitalized from Friday morning until Sunday afternoon. The total bill, for the hospital, doctors, and medicine was $4,120.

When I lived full-time in Mexico, from 2000-2004, I had an interesting experience one spring. Because I have a disease of the corneas, I must wear contact lens. My eyes change shape frequently and, consequently, so must my contact prescription. In the States, a new lens prescription required three to six visits to a specialty clinic, days or weeks of waiting for the contacts, and cost around $1,000. While my insurance helped pay the bill, I was still responsible for a $350 deductible plus a percentage of the total cost.

When my eye problems persisted for months and I found it impossible to return to the States for treatment, I began trying to find an ophthalmologist skilled in corneal problems. After many phone calls, I was referred to an expert in Guadalajara. This man, who spoke English fluently, analyzed my problems in one visit. My vision was 20/60 in one eye and 20/100 in the other (20/20 is considered optimal vision), and the badly damaged lens surfaces were doing corneal damage on a daily basis. He gave me two medications and told me to return the next day to get my contacts.

When I got my new lens, I was amazed and delighted to find my vision was now 20/20! And, what's even more remarkable, the total cost for the doctor's expertise and the contact lens was only $200 US. As I said, health care in Mexico is a bargain!

But no matter whether you decide to insure or not, you will find that you can do some inexpensive self-medicating in Mexico. Antibiotics are available over the counter at reasonable prices. If you've had a couple sinus infections, you know what the symptoms are. In Mexico, you can skip the doctor visit for the prescription and go straight to the pharmacy. That's definitely an advantage. Also, you will find most of your prescription drugs are much cheaper in Mexico. Most visitors stock up on their medical supplies while they're here.

Dental Care

It is possible to find dentists in almost every area of Mexico who are competent and professional. Many have trained in the States and speak English. And, my dentist in Ajijic has more sophisticated equipment than my dentist in North Carolina!

You will also be pleasantly surprised by the cost of dental care. A cleaning costs around 300 pesos, a filling is 350-450 pesos and a root canal, performed by an endodontist, is just 2000-3000 pesos. A crown costs about the same. These prices are the ones charged by English-speaking, US-trained dentists, but you will find lower prices if you use the services of a Mexican-trained dentist. I am not implying that Mexican dentists are inferior. My friends give me wonderful reports on the inexpensive and excellent care they receive. But, until I am proficient in Spanish, I find it easier to use dentists who speak English.

As is always true in a foreign country, asking people for recommendations is the best way to find a doctor or dentist. In Ajijic, the Lake Chapala Society maintains a list of area professionals, and you may find your local expatriate group has a similar list. At LCS, go to the information desk and ask the person on duty for a copy of the doctor/dentist list.   For the cost of the photocopying, you will have a detailed inventory of every professional in the area.

15 DAY TO DAY

House Insurance

Home insurance is not necessary in Mexico because building construction using brick or adobe makes houses impervious to the usual problems, such as fire, that are encountered elsewhere. If you want to ensure the contents of your house or apartment against theft, however, you might want to contact your local insurance company that caters to expatriates in your town.

Security

I choose to do without the annual $150 insurance cost, and prefer, instead, to select houses that seem burglar proof. I look for places with metal grills on all the windows and doors and with high ten-foot high walls surrounding the property. In some houses where I'm unsure about the previous tenant, I will hire a locksmith who replaces the locks for a modest fee that's usually less than 250 pesos.

Any time a service person comes to the fuss about locking up my dog, a Belgiai looks like a German shepherd, telling tl .... my "perro" is "mucho bravo." I want everyone in town to think my dog would attack if an uninvited guest appeared. If you follow the same approach, I doubt you'll have to worry about intruders.

It's important to note, though, that most crimes in Mexico are committed to acquire property and seldom, if ever, is anyone hurt. Someone may want what you have, but he doesn't want to hurt you!

As for **car security**, this is a serious concern. American cars are very much in demand in Mexico and that inevitably leads to theft. Make sure the house or apartment you rent has secure off-street parking, behind a gate you can lock, and use a steering wheel lock. The Club is an example but there are many less expensive brands of steering wheel locks. If that's impossible and you have to park on the street on a regular basis, you may also want to invest in a "kill switch" which disables your car until a hidden button is pressed. Installation costs about 500 pesos in Mexico. That and the steering wheel lock should keep your car safe. By the way, always use anti-theft devices any time you leave your car unattended anywhere in

Mexico. And if you go to a market or fiesta, and a child offers to keep an eye on your car for a few pesos, take him up on the offer. It's worth a couple pesos for peace of mind.

Don't Lose Your Plate!

Don't forget that your license plate is just as vulnerable as your car in certain places in Mexico. Attach the plate with bolts that are difficult to remove and require special tools such as hex keys. You might also try my approach.

Every time I went to visit friends in San Miguel de Allende, the police confiscated my license plate. After I had to pay the police 80 pesos for the third time (No matter how hard I tried, I couldn't seem to park in an area that the police found satisfactory.), I decided to use Super Glue!   My plate has remained with the car ever since.

Internet Service

The Mexican telephone company provides an excellent Internet service called Prodigy that is available in most towns. The dial up service with unlimited hours costs less if paying by the year, rather than by the month. I found the prices for most

Internet services to be about the same as those in the United States.

Telmex also can provide DSL access, including your land line phone cost, for roughly 389 pesos per month. In Mexico, call this toll-free number for more information: 01-800-123-2222

CD that makes installation on your computer relatively easy. Once installed, the service is as easy to use as any in Canada or the States. Everything is in English, and Hotbot or Google or whatever other search engine you prefer can be your homepage.

Some towns catering to expatriates will provide another Internet service option. Here in Ajijc, Lagunanet services Lakeside with both DSL basic and high speed service. See their prices at this website: http://laguna.com.mx/

Do not forget to protect your computer. It is imperative that you use an Uninterruptible Power Supply (a surge protector with a battery back-up), the best you can find, for your computer. Mexico has frequent fluctuations in power, several blackouts a year, and occasional brownouts. Without a surge protector, you will undoubtedly lose your whole system in a matter of weeks or months. The battery back-up surge protectors are expensive but cheap when you consider the cost of replacing your entire computer.

Television

There are usually four choices in most large Mexican towns for subscription television. You can arrange for the Mexican cable service, satellite reception, Direct TV, or Star Choice.

In the Lake Chapala area, if your rental house is already wired for cable, you must pay an initiation fee and a certain amount each month thereafter. You will receive almost fifty stations, at least a dozen in English, including CNN and quite a few movies-only stations. You cannot receive the US network stations ABC, CBS, or NBC.

The other three choices require special equipment: a satellite dish and receiver, and special wiring. In most towns, a local company can supply everything you need. The prices for these services vary considerably depending on what stations you select, but, depending on your choices, you can receive the US networks, Canadian programming (available only with Star

Choice), and many specialty channels such as Discovery, HGTV, the History Channel, the Learning Channel, Food, and sports stations.

Just as you must use a surge protector on your computer, it's imperative to protect your television also. While you don't need quite as expensive a model as you use on the computer, you will still want to have an adequate one to prevent damage from power surges and outages.

Automobile Costs

A gallon of gas, sold by the liter in Mexico, costs about the same as in Arizona. You will be pleasantly surprised, though, by the cost of routine service or major car repairs. An oil change usually costs less than $20, and a flat tire is repaired for $5. While living in Mexico in 2003, I had a new clutch put in my old VW van for less than $300.

Even if you have car problems on the road, you will probably be delighted by the repair costs. My son, daughter-in-law and I had car trouble on the way back from Puerto Vallarta in February, 2003, and we found ourselves in a small Mexican town where no one spoke English. Since we had absolutely no idea why the van suddenly stopped wanting to go uphill, we simply threw ourselves on the mercy of the mechanic. I pantomimed the problem, used the 25 Spanish words I know, and hoped for the best. After an hour's wait, while Joel got a 30 pesos haircut across the street and Courtney and I drank sodas, the mechanic showed me the filthy gas filter he'd replaced, pantomimed that he'd sent his son to the car parts store, twice, to get the right part, and that we were now ready to go. We paid him 250 pesos and got home in record time!

If you experience car trouble on one of the *cuotas*, toll highways, in Mexico you are really in luck. The government provides those "green angels" I mentioned earlier. They are mobile mechanics who patrol the roads to offer free repair service, provide gas or water, or find tow service for hapless motorists. Just pull off to the side of the road and wait. It shouldn't be long before a green truck comes your way.

Because a lot of the roads you will travel are not well-maintained, however, you want to be careful about the car you drive to Mexico. Cobblestone streets and potholes eventually damage every car, but wreak havoc immediately on sports or luxury cars. As I mentioned earlier, it's a good idea to take extra belts with you, but it might also be wise to check with your mechanic to see how readily parts will be available for your particular model.

Personal Care

For me, one of the joys of living in Mexico is that formerly prohibitively expensive services are now within my reach. I'd never had a pedicure before moving to Ajijic, but at a mere 100 pesos, I now indulge myself at least once a month. Manicures cost about the same amount and haircuts can be obtained for between 40-100 pesos, depending on the salon you choose. Most salons also provide massage by licensed therapists for 180-220 pesos per hour.

I treated myself to a pedicure and facial one recent summer. I enjoyed one and a half hours of pampering for only 401 pesos ($32). The same services in San Diego would have cost $160!

16 QUALITY OF LIFE

John and his wife Margaret planned to move south of the border as soon as they retired. For two years, they spent every vacation exploring Mexico, took Spanish lessons, culled their belongings, held yard sales, and longed for the day they'd be moving. During their last visit to San Miguel de Allende they'd finally bought their dream house.

When they were just months away from the move, John suffered a heart attack, underwent an unsuccessful surgical procedure, and his doctor gave him the unwelcome news that his heart problems meant he had only a few months to live. This was a problem they never expected and making a decision about the future was excruciatingly difficult. After agonizing over their options, they decided to go ahead with their plans, knowing there was excellent medical care in a nearby city, and hope for the best. With a laugh, John told me that they made the move twelve years ago!

I met Dee and Al, an affable couple in their early sixties, one morning at Laguna's Bed 'n' Brunch. While we enjoyed what surely must be the best pancakes in the world, they told me their story.

While both of them were perfectly happy with their jobs near Waco, Texas, the doctor had told Dee she must retire. She was using a respirator machine several times a day and spending close to $500 a month on medicine to control her asthma problems. The physician told her to travel around the country and find a place where she felt more comfortable. He told her she simply couldn't go on living in Texas unless she wanted even more health problems.

Dee and Al dutifully followed doctor's orders, bought a small recreation vehicle and a book listing the best places to retire in the United States. They spent the next three months traveling around the country, stopping in all the recommended spots. They didn't have much luck, though. While they found some delightful towns, Dee was still taking as much medicine as before and still using her respirator.

More as a whim than anything else, they decided to visit some friends who were spending the winter in Ajijic. They were charmed by the village, but absolutely amazed by Dee's response to it. Within 24-hours, she'd stopped using the respirator. Within three days, she no longer needed any medication!

They'd found the right place at last! They rented a three-bedroom house in La Floresta, a subdivision of Ajijic, for $500 and couldn't wait to move in.

When I first traveled in Mexico, I heard stories like this over and over again. I finally began to realize that even though Mexico could not provide the Fountain of Youth, there were still good reasons to expect a healthier life in this country.

The **climate** where most expatriates live is the best in the world. Balmy days and refreshingly cool nights all year-round mean that no one has to contend with the extremes of snowy winters or stifling summers. Because there's no heating or air conditioning recycling stale air, all you breathe is fresh air tempered by crisp mountain breezes. Most homes have outdoor terrace rooms where people curl up to read a book in the afternoon and entertain dinner guests at night.

Mexico is also a healthier place to live because of **the food.** Fresh fruit and vegetables are always in season and taste so much better in Mexico that you eat more of them. In fact, unlike North American produce that is picked green and allowed to ripen in transit, Mexican produce is picked at its peak and sold in the market the very next day. And little or no preservatives are used in processed food which means you're ingesting fewer chemicals.

You will find that life is so much **more enjoyable** because you finally have time to pursue your hobbies and develop your talents. People who move to Mexico finally have time to prepare the recipes they've been saving from gourmet magazines, put the box of photographs into albums, or garden to their hearts' content in this land where flowers grow all year long. Others develop new interests and discover latent talents when they take a ceramics or watercolor class. There are also innumerable opportunities for volunteer work. Here in Ajijic, the expatriates maintain a school teaching English and computer skills, manage the only library in town for Mexicans, run a housing facility for the elderly, and assist children who were born with handicaps.

For people who love to socialize, there's probably no better place in the world to make friends. People who don't work have more time to party! But, even more than that, expatriates, because of their adventurous natures, seem more gregarious than their American/Canadian counterparts. Then, too, expatriates find themselves thrown into a world where they must cooperate and share information in order to survive.

There's **less stress** here, too. If you can adjust to the *manana* attitude and remember that *manana* doesn't necessarily mean tomorrow, it just means not today, you will realize that everything will eventually get done that needs doing and with far less frustration. Rather than worrying, go to the plaza, sit on a bench, and watch village life pass before your eyes. You will see a family out for a stroll, a little boy riding on his father's shoulders while Mom buys her daughter a balloon; you'll notice the teenage girls going one direction in the plaza while the boys pass the other way, all of them casting furtive glances at the ones they like; and you'll see old friends who will sit down with you for a chat because they're in the plaza doing the same thing you're doing—enjoying life!

One of my favorite stories about Mexico was written by an unknown author. I think it best sums up the values that make the Mexican people so endearing and the country such a wonderful place to live.

An American businessman stood at the pier of a coastal Mexican village where a fisherman had just docked. Inside the small boat were several yellow fin tunas. The American complimented the Mexican on the quality of and size of his fish and asked how long it had taken to catch them.

"Only a little while," the fisherman said.

The American asked why he hadn't stayed out longer and caught more fish. The Mexican replied that he had enough to meet his family's immediate needs.

The American then asked, "But what do you do with the rest of your time?"

The fisherman said, "I sleep late, fish a little, play with my children, take a siesta with my wife, Maria, and stroll into the village each evening where I sip wine and play guitar with my amigos. I have a full and busy life, senor."

The American scoffed. "I am a Harvard MBA and could help you. You should spend more time fishing and with the proceeds, buy a bigger boat. With the proceeds from the bigger boat, you could buy several boats. Eventually, you would have a fleet of fishing boats. Instead of selling your catch to a middleman, you would sell directly to the processor, eventually opening your own cannery. You would need to leave this small coastal fishing village and move to Mexico City, then Los Angeles, and eventually New York City, where you will run your expanding enterprise."

The Mexican fisherman asked, "But, senor, how long will all this take?"

"Fifteen to twenty years."

"But what then, senor?"

The American laughed and said, "That's the best part. When the time is right, you would announce an IPO and sell your company stock to the public and become very rich. You would make millions."

"Millions, senor? Then what?"

"Then you would retire. You would move to a small coastal fishing village where you would sleep late, fish a little, play with your kids, take a siesta with your wife, and stroll to the village in the evenings, where you could sip wine and play guitar with your amigos."

I'm not implying that Mexico is Shangri-La, but I think it's closer to paradise than any place you can find in the United States or Canada. Here in this land of majestic mountains and rolling countryside, you will find a gentle people willing to welcome you into their hearts. You will have more time to explore other interests and develop your talents because you have more freedom, better health, less stress, and someone else to take care of mundane chores. The low cost of living allows you to splurge on luxuries that would be prohibitive anywhere else and to take advantage of world-class resorts that are only a few hours' drive away.

So, give it a try. Use this book to make a painless and inexpensive move to the "land of perpetual spring." I think you'll be glad you did!

ABOUT THE AUTHOR

Dru Pearson fell in love with travel when her parents took her to Camp Corbly when she was three months old. She's suffered from wanderlust ever since.

Read her book, *Europe on a Dime: Five-Star Travel on a One-Star Budget,* and take a look at her blog, http://tightwadtravel.blogspot.com for frugal travel tips in other parts of the world.